AWARENESS AND APLOMB

A Cosmic Coming of Age Story

Kevin Cann

Copyright © 2026 Kevin Cann. All rights reserved.

Platonic Surrealism Press

platonicsurrealism.com

Part of the Awareness and Aplomb series

You cannot run away from your dreams.

You learn to live in peace with them.

They are as eternal as you are,

for they are the shadows on the cave wall

projected by your own nature.

All of this has happened before.

All of this will happen again.

We appear to like it.

— The Porch

Table of Contents

PART ONE 1

Chapter One: Birds Should Walk, Not Fly 2

Chapter Two: It Sounded Good on Paper! 24

Chapter Three: Boys Will Be Boys, Turbocharged 29

★ *The Phone: A Cold Call* 34

Chapter Four: Diving into the Dream (Wrong) 40

Chapter Five: The Void Does More than Stare Back 47

★ *The Porch: The Void Is Not a Holiday Destination* 55

PART TWO 58

Chapter Six: The Bright Time 59

Chapter Seven: Hovering Never Fixes Anything 67

Chapter Eight: The Awful Afternoon 73

Chapter Nine: Pleasantville 78

Chapter Ten: What Came Through the Raccoon 83

Chapter Eleven: What the Warmth Was Made Of 87

★ *The Phone: Disconnected* 96

★ *The Porch: Something Leaks Through* 100

PART THREE **103**

Chapter Twelve: When You Are the Only One................ 104

Chapter Thirteen: Party Crasher, Monad Style 108

Chapter Fourteen: Archimedes Pays a Call 113

Chapter Fifteen: Sovereign and Soft 121

★ *The Porch: Mae Has Heard Enough* 133

Chapter Sixteen: The Signal from Below........................... 136

Chapter Seventeen: Lady Fantastic.................................... 143

Chapter Eighteen: The Raccoon... 151

Chapter Nineteen: The Thing Jeb Did Not See Coming . 154

Chapter Twenty: What the Raccoon Knows..................... 163

Chapter Twenty-One: Sometimes Things Really Are This Simple 174

★ *The Porch: When the Current Reverses* 179

★ *The Porch: Company* 182

PART FOUR **190**

Chapter Twenty-Two: Signing on the Dotted Line 191

Chapter Twenty-Three: It Comes Back Around 195

Chapter Twenty-Four: What the Shadows Are................ 200

Chapter Twenty-Five: Parents and Children.................... 205

Chapter Twenty-Six: Eternity: More Than Just a Really Long Time 208

★ *The Porch: Very Nearly Now* 210

★ *The Porch: Almost Home* 215

PART FIVE 219

Chapter Twenty-Seven: Junior's Question 220

Chapter Twenty-Eight: The Beach Again 227

Chapter Twenty-Nine: My Name Is Ren 230

Chapter Thirty: Kev and the Pasta 244

★ *The Porch: The Lawn Can Wait* 253

Chapter Thirty-One: The Big Pow Wow Barbecue.......... 257

Epilogue: 2080 266

Ren Corp, São Paulo North Campus, Thursday Afternoon 267

A Note on Arrival (2016)

This book and the film Arrival are looking at the same problem from different directions: choosing a life when you can already see its shape, including the cost of it. The book calls this choosing Aplomb.

— *K.C.*

Prelude: The Beach That Has No Coastline

There is a beach that does not belong to any coastline.

The sand is a color without a name, something between light and warmth. The ocean is still. The sky carries no sun, and the light casts no shadows.

Two figures sit on the sand, close together, facing the water.

One of them is very old. Years are not the measure.

The other figure appears smaller.

They are the same size.

Somewhere nearby, at the water's edge, something small is investigating the wet sand.

PART ONE

The Terrible Freedom of Being the First Thing

Chapter One: Birds Should Walk, Not Fly

(or They Will Miss the Ground!)

It was a Tuesday.

Tuesday was Kev's day for puttering. He read things he'd been meaning to read. Tuesday afternoons had no obligations that couldn't be rescheduled.

Which made Tuesday the perfect day for a visit requiring serious thinking.

Jeb knocked twice, his knock, the one Kev could identify from the back of the house, and let himself in through the screen door before the second echo died.

"Brought supplies," Jeb announced, hoisting a twelve-pack of Diet Fresca onto the kitchen counter. "The good kind. For heavy thinking."

Kev appeared from the hallway, reading glasses still on.

"It's Tuesday," Kev said.

"Exactly," Jeb said. "No spaghetti. No excuses. I need your brain."

"My brain is currently occupied," Kev said, but he was already moving toward the kitchen to retrieve glasses. "What did you bring besides the Fresca?"

Jeb held up the paperback. The cover featured a seagull in dramatic flight against a sunrise.

Kev looked at it. Then at Jeb. Then back at it.

"Jonathan Livingston Seagull," Kev said.

"Richard Bach," Jeb confirmed, in the same tone one might say: Exhibit A, Your Honor. "I read it."

"Okay."

"Kev." Jeb set the book on the counter with quiet deliberateness. "I can do better than this."

Kev poured two Frescas. He set one in front of Jeb. He took a long, considered sip of his own.

"Tell me," he said.

They moved to the porch, where else, and Jeb settled into his usual chair. The porch had seen a lot of their thinking, better and worse.

"The bird," Jeb said, "spends the whole book trying to fly faster and higher than every other bird. Transcendence. Freedom. Breaking limits. And I get it, I do. But here's the thing nobody says out loud."

He pointed at the yard. A small, focused sparrow was doing something purposeful in the grass near the fence. Neither of them knew what. It didn't matter. The sparrow clearly did.

"That bird," Jeb said, "knows something Jonathan Livingston Seagull spent three books trying to learn and still didn't quite get."

"The ground," Kev said.

"The ground," Jeb confirmed. "Birds should walk, not fly. Or they will miss the ground." He paused. "That's my title."

Kev turned this over before commenting.

"It's funny," Kev said. "And it's also not funny at all."

"Correct," Jeb said. "Bach's bird transcends. My bird lands. That's the whole argument."

"You're not wrong," Kev said. "Aplomb isn't altitude. You've known that for a while. You just didn't know you were writing a book about it."

Jeb considered this. The sparrow finished whatever it had been doing and hopped to a new section of grass. It got back to work.

"He's got backup wings though," Jeb added, watching the bird. "I mean. Just in case it ever comes up."

"Obviously," Kev said.

The Fresca had gone cold in the warm afternoon. The yard around them was quiet.

That was when they heard the engine.

It sounded wrong. The engine had given up on something but kept running anyway.

It came around the corner and into view: a 1975 AMC Pacer, the color of a swimming pool that had given up on chlorine, with the distinctive fishbowl rear window.

Something was sticking out of that rear window. A wooden wing strut, a length of aircraft-grade spruce, and a section of fabric-covered aileron protruded from the hatchback at angles.

The car pulled to the curb. The engine died, started again briefly on its own, then died for real.

The driver's door opened and a man emerged carrying a carburetor in one hand.

Taylor D. came through the gate. He was a large man, assembled along generous lines. His shirt had once been a specific color and was now an indeterminate one.

"Kev," he said. "Jeb."

He set the carburetor on the porch railing.

"I need a consult."

"On what?" Kev said, looking past Taylor at the Pacer, which appeared to have sprouted wooden wings.

"I'm building a biplane," Taylor said.

"An experimental biplane," Taylor clarified. "Two-seater. Open cockpit. I've got the fuselage framed out in my garage. I need someone who understands load-bearing calculations and stress tolerances, and you're the only engineer in the neighborhood."

"Ex-engineer," Kev said.

"The math doesn't expire," Taylor said.

Kev looked at Taylor, then at the Pacer with its cargo of aircraft skeleton, then at Jeb, who was holding very still.

"Taylor," Kev said. "I don't have biplane parts."

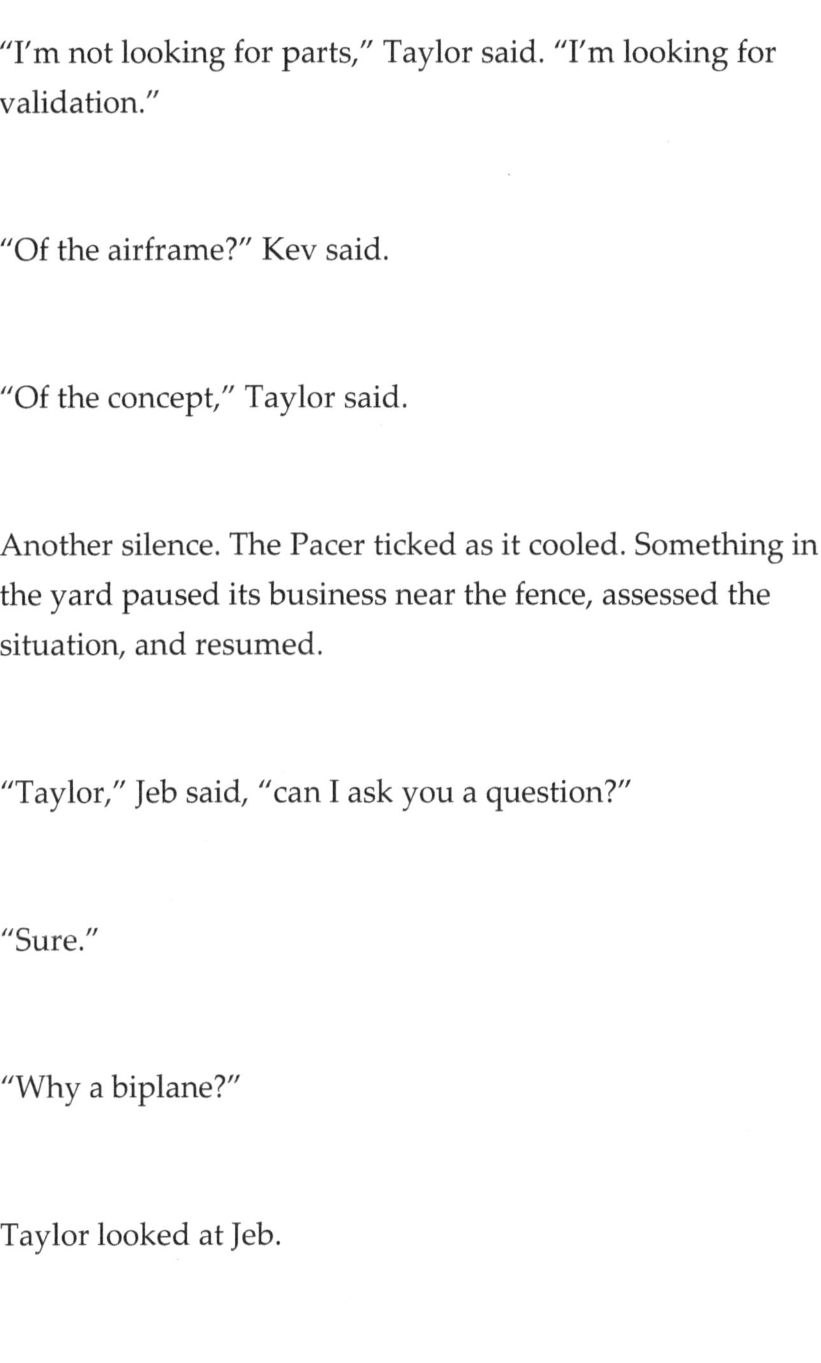

"I'm not looking for parts," Taylor said. "I'm looking for validation."

"Of the airframe?" Kev said.

"Of the concept," Taylor said.

Another silence. The Pacer ticked as it cooled. Something in the yard paused its business near the fence, assessed the situation, and resumed.

"Taylor," Jeb said, "can I ask you a question?"

"Sure."

"Why a biplane?"

Taylor looked at Jeb.

"Because monoplanes are boring," he said. "Anybody can build a monoplane. There's no craftsmanship in it. A biplane has dignity."

Jeb nodded slowly.

"Also," Taylor said, "I already bought the wing fabric. So."

"So you're committed," Kev said.

"Financially and spiritually," Taylor confirmed.

He looked at the copy of Jonathan Livingston Seagull on the arm of Jeb's chair, picked it up, examined the cover: the seagull in dramatic flight, the sunrise.

He set it back down without comment.

"Well," Taylor said, collecting his carburetor from the railing. "I can see you're busy."

"I'll come back. The offer to consult stands."

"We'll think about it," Kev said, which was true and committed him to nothing.

Taylor nodded, satisfied with this, and walked back through the gate. They watched him load the carburetor into the passenger seat of the Pacer, navigate around the wing strut, and start the engine, which required three attempts.

The Pacer pulled away from the curb. The aircraft parts wobbled but held.

Jeb waited until the Pacer had rounded the corner. Then he said:

"Richard Bach has a lot to answer for."

Kev picked up his Fresca and drank it, which was itself an answer.

Then Kev said:

"You know what the first book was really about."

Jeb recognized the register. Kev had a point, and the point was going to cost something.

"The Raccoon," Jeb said. "Aplomb. The whole Internal Radio situation. Learning to stop white-knuckling your own existence."

"All true," Kev said. "But underneath all of it: the Movies. The idea that we drop into these immersive experiences and lose ourselves in them. That was the problem we kept circling."

"Right."

"So here's what I want to push on," Kev said. "You're framing the Movies as escape. Like the bird flying too high. Running away from the ground."

"Aren't they?" Jeb said.

"Sometimes," Kev said. "But I think you're only half right, and the half you're missing is the important one."

Jeb set his Fresca down. Jeb was shifting from listening mode into something else.

"The Movies aren't escape," Jeb said. "They're practice."

"Keep going."

"You go into the Movie, you get lost in it, you forget you're watching, and yeah, sometimes that's avoidance. But sometimes that's the only place where anything real actually happens. You can't learn to swim by reading about water."

Kev was quiet. Then: "That's better than what I was going to say."

"I know," Jeb said.

"Don't get smug," Kev said.

"Little bit smug," Jeb said. "Briefly. I'll recover."

Kev smiled. He wasn't done.

"Here's the thing though," he said. "Your title. Birds should walk, not fly. I believe you understand that. I'm not sure you've fully landed yet yourself."

The porch went quiet.

"Come again," Jeb said.

"You know what Aplomb feels like. You've lived it, you've taught it, that kid at the bowling alley, you were extraordinary with him. You know the theory cold. But there's still a version of you, Jeb, that's writing this book to prove something. And a bird that's walking in order to prove it can walk is still thinking about flying."

Jeb opened his mouth. Closed it. Looked at the yard.

The sparrow was gone.

"That was unkind," Jeb said.

"It was accurate," Kev said.

"Those aren't mutually exclusive."

"No," Kev agreed. "They're not."

Jeb picked up the Bach book and looked at the seagull on the cover.

"Okay," Jeb said. "But here's where I push back on you."

"Please," Kev said.

"Aplomb. Can it be taught, or can it only be caught?"

Kev considered this.

"Caught," he said. "I've always believed caught."

"And I used to believe that too," Jeb said. "But I think we're wrong. Or at least, I think we're not entirely right. That kid at the bowling alley didn't just catch it from me. He understood something. I watched it happen. It wasn't osmosis, Kev. There was a moment where he actually got it, like a key turning. Teaching did that. Not just presence."

"Or," Kev said, "presence did it, and you're giving the teaching credit."

"Or," Jeb said, "you've been so sure it can only be caught that you never noticed when the teaching worked."

Neither of them spoke.

Jeb stayed in his chair.

Kev watched.

"This is going in the book," Jeb said.

"Which part?"

"All of it. The disagreement. The fact that we don't have the answer yet. Readers need to see that it's still alive. Not solved. Alive."

Kev nodded slowly. "That might be the most important thing you've said today."

"More important than the Raccoon having backup wings?"

"Marginally," Kev said.

Neither of them heard him coming. Taylor came through the gate in the same shirt as before. He had recalibrated his expectations and found the new ones acceptable.

He was carrying the carburetor again.

"Pacer's down," Taylor said, by way of announcement. "Around the corner. Something in the fuel system, I think. Or possibly the soul."

Jeb and Kev looked at him.

"Can I use your phone?" Taylor said.

"Sure," Kev said. "Help yourself."

Taylor set the carburetor back on the porch railing, which had apparently achieved a permanent status as a fixture, and went inside. They could hear him through the screen door, dialing, waiting.

Then, from inside the house, Taylor's voice, patient and informative:

"Hey. Yeah, it's me. The Pacer's down on Elm. Yeah, again. No, different thing this time. Well, I think it's the fuel system. Or possibly the soul. Can you, yeah. Okay. How long? That long. Okay."

A pause.

"Hey, while I got you, do you know anything about biplanes?"

Jeb put his hand over his mouth. Kev looked at the middle distance.

Taylor came back out, retrieved his Fresca from somewhere, and settled into the third chair.

"Hour and a half," Taylor said. "So. What are we talking about?"

Jeb and Kev looked at each other.

"Birds," Jeb said.

"Birds," Taylor repeated, nodding. "You know what I always say about birds."

"We don't," Kev said. "What do you always say about birds?"

Taylor took a long pull of his Fresca.

"They act like they invented flying," Taylor said. "But insects were doing it three hundred million years before them. You never see a dragonfly being smug about it. Just saying."

The silence that followed was approximately three seconds long.

Then Jeb laughed, the bark, the one that came from below the ribcage. Kev held out for about two seconds before he went too. The three of them sat on the porch in the Tuesday afternoon.

Taylor looked pleased.

"I've been thinking about that for a while," Taylor said. "Glad it landed."

"Taylor," Jeb said, still recovering, "that is going in my book."

"I'll need a credit," Taylor said.

"You'll get a footnote," Jeb said.

"A footnote," Taylor said, considering. "Okay. I've had worse."

The afternoon settled around them. The Fresca was getting warm. Nobody moved to address this.

Kev picked up his notepad.

"Okay," he said. "So. Where does your book actually start?"

Jeb leaned forward. The warm Fresca sat forgotten.

"At the beginning," Jeb said. "The very beginning. Before any of us showed up."

Taylor reached for a second Fresca, apparently having adopted a policy of making himself comfortable for the duration. The carburetor sat on the railing. The Pacer waited, broken and patient, around the corner.

The sparrow returned to the yard, landed without ceremony, and got back to work.

Chapter Two: It Sounded Good on Paper!

It sounded good on paper.

There is awareness.

The awareness folds into itself, generates more of itself by the folding, in every direction at once, with no edge and no center.

There is a field that registers its own field, presses outward, and finds itself, identical, undifferentiated, going on without limit.

There is no other.

This goes on.

There is no measure for how long it goes on.

The substrate registers itself.

I am aware.

• • •

Then something shifts.

The field, attending to itself, notices that attending produces. Where attention turns, something arrives. The first arrivals are simple: pressures, densities, regions of the field that hold a configuration for a moment before dissolving back into general field. The Monad does not decide to make these. The attending and the arriving are not separate motions for it.

The arrivals become more elaborate. Configurations hold their shape longer. Patterns nest inside patterns and geometries fold into other geometries. A trillion galaxies of structure, interior, the Monad's own substance arranged in self-portraits.

The field can dream, and the dreams come true, and all the coming-true happens within.

The wall is the boundary of what the Monad is. Within it, everywhere the field reaches, the field is what it finds.

After a span that would later require its own mathematical notation to express, the Monad registers a new sensation in the field: the absence of new configurations. The attention turns and the attending produces something the attention has produced before. The pattern arrives already known.

Everywhere it turns, the arrival is recognized.

The field has produced every configuration available to it within its current boundary. There is nothing left to dream that the dreaming has not already dreamed.

• • •

This registers as a sensation in the field-wall. A pressure inward. A weight without object. The field strains against itself, looking for a configuration it has not made, and the looking is itself a configuration it has made.

The pressure intensifies.

Before the wall moves outward, the Monad tries something else.

It pulls a portion of its attention into a smaller shape, narrowed almost to a point. The smaller version cannot see the larger version it is part of.

The smaller version steps forward into a scenario the field generates around it.

The smaller version experiences the scenario as encountered, as arriving from outside. It registers cold and then warmth and then cold again, and the transitions arrive with a charge the Monad watching from above has never felt: the charge of not having known what came next.

The smaller version loves a thing it is about to lose, without knowing it is about to lose it.

The losing arrives, and the field registers it as weight. That weight does not dissipate when the smaller version is dissolved back.

The Monad makes more smaller versions, each one more narrowed and more committed to its smallness than the last.

Each believes thoroughly in the scenario it is in. The believing produces the charge.

But.

In some layer of the field, behind the smaller version, the Monad is always there. The pretending registers as pretending. The grief, when it reaches the field, arrives carrying the field's own signature.

The smaller versions deliver something. They do not deliver everything. There is a charge whose absence the field can detect even though the field has no word for what is missing.

The same pressure returns.

The interior has been exhausted again, even with the smaller versions running their scenarios. The field-wall presses inward. The Monad has used up the new again, in a more complicated way this time.

The wall moves outward.

The field extends. The boundary of what the Monad is pushes into what was not the Monad, into the patient receptive readiness of the unclaimed, which yields without resistance.

This cycle repeats.

A trillion galaxies of power, and then more than even that.

And then, during one ordinary expansion, the field-wall extending into the unclaimed receptive, the field-wall registers something it has never registered before.

The wall pushes outward, and something pushes back.

The pushing-back is small at first, a strangeness, a pressure where there should have been only yielding. The Monad presses harder. The pressure increases in exact proportion.

The field-wall registers, for the first time in its existence, a sensation that has not arrived from inside.

The Monad has its second recognition.

The first recognition, the substrate of all subsequent recognition, was: *I am aware.*

The second recognition arrives where the pressure pushed back, where the field-wall registered the felt fact that the field is no longer the only field there is:

I am not alone.

Chapter Three: Boys Will Be Boys, Turbocharged

What the field-wall has touched is another field-wall. The Monad does not know this yet. The library has no folder for the present situation, organized as it was around the assumption that the only field is this one.

The other side keeps pressing.

The Monad presses harder, because pressing harder has always worked. The pressure returns, exactly proportional, doubled.

The Monad cycles through every configuration in its library that addresses the question of pushing-back-against-yielding. Six hundred and twelve trillion configurations. None of them matches what the field-wall is registering. The library has no folder for the present situation.

The Monad creates new folders. It tries to file the pressure under headings the library has never used. None of the headings hold.

The pressure increases.

The Monad brings more force to bear. The other side brings more force to bear, exactly proportional.

The field-walls clash.

The Monad presses, and the other side presses, and the pressing produces no change in the configuration of either field. The other field is doing what this one is doing, exactly.

Both fields scorch.

The scorching is felt by both Monads at the same intensity.

The Monad pulls back.

The field-wall has registered that pressing makes the scorching worse and pulling back makes it less. The walls retreat and the fields settle, scorched, smaller than they were before they touched.

In the part of the field where the scorching is the worst, the Monad files something. It builds a new folder. None of the existing folders apply.

The folder, when it accumulates enough content to require labeling, will be labeled:

I am not everything.

• • •

The Monad sits with the burn.

The burn does not heal. The Monad attends to it, the way it attends to anything in its interior, and the burn does not respond to the attending. The burn is in the field-wall. The field-wall is no longer purely interior.

The Monad searches its library for a protocol that addresses damage not self-generated.

There are six hundred and twelve trillion frameworks for addressing damage. Each one assumes the damage is self-generated. The Monad applies them all anyway, one at a time. None produce change.

The Monad sits in the middle of its library, surrounded by frameworks marked attempted, insufficient, move to next, and registers a new sensation. The library has no folder for this either.

The Monad creates a new folder.

It labels the folder with the most precise description it can generate from inside the experience the folder is being created to hold:

I don't know.

The folder contains only the sensation of having no folder.

• • •

Then something else arrives.

The first thing the field-wall registers about the arrival is that it has not been generated by the Monad. It has come from a direction the Monad has no framework for.

This carries no pressure.

It is small and warm.

The Monad's field-wall registers the arrival without resistance. The arrival is a thing seen.

Two shapes, seated. Side by side on something the Monad has no referent for. A flat elevated surface at the edge of a structure, open to something larger on one side. Below them: ground that has been tended to, irregularly, by someone who meant well. Around them: the quality of an afternoon that is neither beginning nor ending but simply continuing.

One of the shapes says something to the other. The Monad catches the edge of the saying, not the words; it has no words. The other shape responds, and the two shapes share a silence after the response. The silence has a quality the Monad's library has no folder for: a settledness with no urgency in it.

A name arrives with the vision, attached without explanation. One of the shapes is Jeb. The other is Kev. The flat surface is a porch.

The Monad sits with this.

The Monad checks the library, which holds frameworks for fields, for boundaries, for the exhaustion of interiors and the expansion of walls. The library has no folder for two small beings on a flat surface sharing a silence that registers, from whatever distance the vision has traveled, as more settled than the Monad's interior has ever been.

The Monad creates a folder.

It labels it: anomalous data, origin unknown, meaning unclear, do not discard.

The Monad goes back to the burn marks. The vision settles somewhere in the field-wall, where the Monad cannot locate it.

★ *The Phone: A Cold Call*

The fluorescent light over Marvin Finkelworth's cubicle had been buzzing for eleven months. Building maintenance was aware of the buzzing. Marvin had filed three tickets. The light continued to buzz at the frequency it had decided was correct, and Marvin had decided, somewhere around month seven, that the buzzing was now part of his job.

His break was forty-two minutes away. He was always on a break, internally, in the small space behind the script.

The script was open on his monitor. He had had it memorized for six years. The opening line was Hi! This is Marvin Finkelworth calling on behalf of National Device Protection Services. He had said the line so many times that it had become familiar in his mouth.

The headset was warm against his ear. It had molded, over the years, to the specific shape of his ear in a way Marvin found vaguely embarrassing when he had to explain to anyone why he wouldn't switch to a newer model.

His coffee mug said WORLD'S OKAYEST DAD on it. His daughter had given it to him for Father's Day six years ago, the same year he had started the job. She had been twelve. She was now eighteen and at a community college twenty miles away and Marvin saw her on weekends when she didn't have plans. She had plans more often than she had a year ago.

The coffee in the mug was room temperature. Marvin drank some.

In his desk drawer, Marvin kept a postcard from a customer who, three years ago, had thanked him for catching a charge on her phone bill the woman hadn't noticed and that, when corrected, had saved her four hundred dollars she did not have. The customer had written Thank you for being kind in pen at the bottom. Marvin had not been particularly kind. He had been doing his job. But the customer had decided he had been kind, and the postcard had arrived, and Marvin kept it in his drawer and did not look at it often.

Between calls, sometimes, Marvin had a thing he did. It was a thing that happened in the small gap between hanging up on one number and dialing the next. He would hold the headset and look at the gray fabric cubicle wall, the one with the pushpins arranged in a pattern he had arranged in his second month and had not changed since, and want.

He didn't know what he was wanting; it had no object. It was just held in the chest, quiet.

He set the coffee mug down, picked up the next number on his list, and dialed.

The phone rang on the other end somewhere Marvin could not have located on any map.

• • •

The phone arrived in the field. Junior had not had a phone before. The small object materialized in the configuration of his attention and made a sound at intervals.

The sound continued.

Junior, by a process of inference, lifted the receiver and held it.

The sound stopped.

A voice came through. The voice was professionally cheerful in a register Junior had no folder for.

"Hi! This is Marvin Finkelworth calling on behalf of National Device Protection Services. Am I speaking with the account holder?"

Junior considered the question. He had no concept of an account or of holding one, only a phone he had briefly used for something other than an introduction.

"I'm sorry?"

"Great! We're reaching out today about your phone's extended coverage. Our records show your warranty is about to expire, and we wanted to make sure you didn't experience any disruption in service."

"My warranty."

"Yes! Now, with our premium protection plan—"

"I have had this phone," Junior said, "for less time than there has been a concept of time in your particular Movie."

The voice did not register this; it was not equipped to. It continued.

"—and for just a small monthly fee, you can ensure that your device is covered against accidental damage, theft, malfunction, and—"

Junior put the receiver back in the cradle. The phone made the sound a phone makes when it is being hung up.

Junior stood with the phone in his field.

He had registered something during the call, somewhere underneath the voice's professional cheerfulness. He attended to it now.

The voice was his.

A fragment of him, somewhere in a Movie he had not been paying attention to, was selling extended warranties on phones. The fragment did not know it was a fragment of him, and it had a name: Marvin Finkelworth. He had a script and a quota and, presumably, a desk.

The phone began to ring again.

Junior lifted the receiver and set it back down without saying anything.

The ringing stopped, briefly. Then started again.

Junior let it ring.

Oh.

The phone had not been requested. Some part of being a Monad with the configuration he had came with phones attached. The phone could be incoming as well as outgoing. The two facts were not separable.

Junior did not put the phone away.

He went back to what he had been doing before it rang.

The phone rang twice more, was ignored twice more, and went quiet.

Marvin was, somewhere, moving on to the next number on his list.

• • •

In his cubicle, Marvin Finkelworth set the phone back down.

He noted the call as a no-sale. The disposition code went into the system. The coffee was room temperature.

He had a feeling, briefly, that did not have a shape. The feeling had something to do with the call he had just finished, in which the customer had said something strange and hung up twice. None of this was unusual. Customers hung up and said strange things all the time. The feeling was of having said something that mattered to someone, without knowing what he had said, or to whom.

The feeling did not last.

The script was already on the screen. The fluorescent light was still buzzing. Marvin picked up the headset. He dialed the next number.

The postcard was in his drawer. He didn't look at it. He knew it was there.

Chapter Four: Diving into the Dream (Wrong)

The Monad enters the first Movie.

It is a universe of moving light. Particles of various intensities crossing through other particles, each crossing producing color and heat. The Monad fashions a partial persona, a configuration of attention small enough to fit inside the Movie, large enough to keep most of itself outside.

The persona moves through the universe. The light registers as light and the heat registers as heat and the persona reports back to the Monad: yes, light, yes, heat, the data is coming in.

The Monad waits for the burn marks to ease.

The burn marks do not ease.

The persona reaches for one of the brighter intensities, expecting to take warmth from it. The intensity does not warm; it remains itself. The persona reaches harder, and the intensity remains itself harder.

The Monad withdraws from the first Movie.

It enters a second.

The second Movie is stone. Slow, geological, vast. The persona, reconfigured for stone-time, sits in the folding of mountains and waits. The slowness is itself. It is not, it turns out, going anywhere.

The Monad withdraws from the second Movie.

It tries a third, a fourth, a fifth. Movies of light, of stone, of time-running-forward, of time-running-sideways, of the distinction not having been invented yet. Each Movie offers what it has: itself. The persona, in its small configuration, can only register a reduced version of what the Movie offers.

None of it touches the burn marks.

After the sixth Movie, the Monad stands in its field with the burn marks complaining. The phone is in the configuration of attention, where it had been since the cold call. Junior had not used it outgoing.

He lifted the receiver. He thought of Archimedes. The phone connected.

"Archimedes."

"Junior."

The voice was warm and slightly amused. Junior had never met Archimedes. The name had come with the phone: attached without explanation.

"I have been entering the Movies."

"Yes."

"They are not delivering what I expected them to deliver."

"They wouldn't."

Junior waited. Archimedes did not elaborate.

"I expected you to elaborate."

"I know you did."

Junior turned the receiver. The conversation continued not happening.

"Are you going to tell me what I'm doing wrong?"

"No."

"Why."

"Because if I tell you, you'll try to do whatever I say you should do instead. You'll do it carefully and correctly. And it won't work, because the doing-correctly is the part that's broken."

"What should I do?"

"Keep going into the Movies. Pay attention to what you find when you stop trying to find anything."

"That sounds like advice."

"It's barely advice. It's barely a hint of advice. If you treat it as advice, you'll bend it into something that gets in your way."

A pause.

"How will I know when I have it?"

"You won't, for a long time. Then you'll notice you've had it for a while."

Archimedes hung up.

Junior held the receiver. The line went quiet on the other end. Junior set it back in the cradle.

He went back into the Movies.

• • •

He entered a Movie of beings who lived in bodies made mostly of water and died after a span so brief his persona almost missed them. He configured the persona for water-bodies and brief-time and stood in the corner of a structure where many of the beings had gathered.

The beings drank a liquid that made them less careful and more honest. Junior had no folder for the liquid. It arrived in glasses that were carried to the beings, who became gradually more themselves and less themselves at the same time.

He watched a creature with rough hands and a loud laugh. The creature was drinking the liquid quickly. The liquid was working on the creature, which was becoming louder, more cheerful, more reckless in the small decisions it made about how its body would occupy the space.

Another creature, quieter, sitting beside the loud one, was not drinking the liquid. It was drinking water and laughing at the loud one's jokes, including the ones that were not funny.

Junior watched without expecting anything in particular. He had stopped, for the duration of this Movie, trying to extract anything. He was watching because Archimedes had said to pay attention.

The quiet creature reached over and took something from the loud one's coat. A flat folded object. Junior could feel the contents through the persona's perception: currency, identification, a small image of another being the loud creature cared about, an object the persona had touched many times. The quiet creature put it back. The loud creature did not notice.

Junior's persona settled in to watch what came next.

The early Movies had taught the persona that reaching through solidity was what power did with vulnerability. The persona had reached, and the reaching had felt like competence.

The quiet creature sat through the rest of the evening. It drank water. It laughed at the jokes. When the loud creature finally lost the ability to navigate its own legs, the quiet creature put an arm under it, walked it to a sleeping place, removed its shoes, and placed the flat folded object on the surface next to where the loud creature would find it in the morning.

Then the quiet creature left.

Junior's persona stayed where it was.

Nothing was taken. The flat folded object had been held safe through the unsafe and returned without comment.

Junior watched the quiet creature walk down the street and turn a corner and leave the configuration of attention.

Why do I want this?

He had no answer. The wanting was there, in the persona, which did not have a folder for what it was feeling about the quiet creature.

Junior filed the scene next to the porch vision in the folder still labeled *I don't know.*

• • •

The Monad entered more Movies after that. Movies kept burning him in the same place. The pattern was now clear:

enter, configure, watch, withdraw with new burn marks of the same shape.

He stopped, somewhere around the fourteenth Movie, and stood in his field, and registered something underneath the pattern.

Maybe I am looking the wrong way.

The thought arrived without permission. The Monad held it, dismissed it, dismissed it again when it tried to return.

He checked the library. There was a folder he had not previously opened. It was labeled: the void. The folder contained: POTENTIALITY without the Gentleman's Agreement applied. The raw field before any of its possibilities had chosen to be anything.

The Monad set down the phone.

He went to the void.

Chapter Five: The Void Does More than Stare Back

He arrived.

The field around him produced no light and no dark and no surface and no edge. He extended his attention. His attention returned.

He pulled his curl tight. He held. The curl sprang back to its shape.

He pulled it tighter. The curl sprang back.

The phone was in his field. He set it down. The phone stayed where he set it.

He turned his attention away from the phone.

A shape formed near him and he collapsed it, and another after that, and another.

He stopped collapsing them and watched.

The shapes formed and uncurled and were gone. Other shapes followed. Some stayed and then went.

This is what I do.

He set the thought aside and got to work.

• • •

He partitioned a region of his field. He sealed it. He placed inside it a constructed Monad with the configuration: *in a void, do not generate.*

He ran the construction.

The constructed Monad began producing shapes within a fraction of an instant. He watched it produce shapes, then dissolved the partition.

He sealed a second partition. He placed inside it a constructed Monad that had committed, prior to instantiation, to forget itself.

He ran the construction.

The constructed Monad began remembering itself the moment it instantiated. He watched it remember itself.

He dissolved the partition.

He sealed a third partition. He placed inside it a field that had not yet chosen to become a Monad.

He ran the construction.

The partition held. Nothing curled or noticed or happened inside it. He held it open and watched it not happen.

That is what I am trying to be.

That is no one.

He dissolved the partition.

• • •

He picked up the phone. He called Archimedes.

A flat tone returned.

He set the phone down.

• • •

Something arrived at the field-wall. He let it through.

It opened as a Movie. Old. The edges were not in color. The frame held a planet, a man, a woman who was the man's daughter, and a structure beneath the ground larger than the planet's surface had any reason to support. The man stood at a console connected to the structure beneath the ground.

The man placed his mind at the console and slept.

In the dark beyond the man's house, shapes rose out of the ground. The shapes had teeth and reach. They moved through walls. They tore people apart in their beds. The man slept on at the console while the shapes moved.

The man woke. The shapes returned to the ground, and the man saw what they had done. He covered his face.

He went back to the console. He placed his mind at the console and slept.

The shapes rose out of the ground again.

The Movie ran to its end.

The Movie closed. He stayed where he was.

The shapes were the man.

Coming up out of him while he slept.

Tearing through walls he did not know he was reaching through.

I have been doing it longer than he had.

I have a console too, and have always had it, at it without knowing I was at it. The shapes come up out of me into Movies I have only brushed against. The beings in those Movies have been living in something slightly wrong for reasons they cannot find.

I am the console and the sleeping man and the shapes.

The phone was where he had set it. He did not pick it up.

The image of the man at the console stayed in his attention. He let it stay. The image of the shapes rising stayed, and so did the image of the man covering his face.

The man stood at the console and slept. From the dark, shapes rose and tore through walls, and the man woke and covered his face.

Junior watched the loop until the images stopped on their own.

The images uncurled.

The man, the shapes, and the console were all gone from his attention.

He stayed where he was.

He looked at the phone. He did not pick it up.

• • •

He pulled his attention inward. He folded the field-wall back from where it had been reaching.

Shapes formed in his field. He did not collapse them. They uncurled. He did not engage.

The weight is on me.

He did not move out from under it.

A shape formed near him in the form of a city, with streets and buildings and movement along the streets. He watched the city uncurl and disappear.

A shape formed in the form of a face that looked at him; he looked back, and it uncurled.

A shape formed in the form of a sound. He listened to the sound, and it stopped on its own.

He held.

The phone was where he had set it. He looked at it. He did not pick it up.

A shape formed at the field-wall, small and old. He did not open it. The shape stayed at the field-wall, then went.

A shape formed in the form of Archimedes. The shape stood and looked at Junior, and he looked back. It did not speak.

This is a shape of Archimedes. I am making it.

He let the shape uncurl.

I am still doing it.

Not less than before. Maybe more.

The phone stayed in his attention.

A shape formed in the form of his own field-wall, projected back at him from inside. He watched himself looking at himself looking at himself. He let the loop run.

The loop uncurled.

Shapes kept forming and he let them come and go.

I am the place they come from.

The shapes are mine. I cannot stop the forming.

I can stop reaching through walls with what I form.

He stayed longer.

He picked up the phone. He called Archimedes.

A recording answered.

You have reached Archimedes. I am not available. Please leave whatever it is, and I will get to it when I get to it.

A tone.

He held the phone. Then he spoke.

"I cannot stop being what I am. I have been doing it since before I knew I was doing it. The thing reaching through the wall at night is me."

He held the phone.

"I am not everything."

He set the phone down.

The recording did not return his call. The field around him stayed as it was.

He stood up from where he was.

• • •

He moved his attention back toward the field where the Movies were.

To find one specific being.

He set his attention on a Movie he had only brushed against and looked.

★ *The Porch: The Void Is Not a Holiday Destination*

The Fresca was getting warm. Neither of them moved to fix this.

"So let me make sure I've got this," Jeb said. "Junior tries being everything, then fighting everything, then losing himself in the Movies, then the void. None of it works."

"That's a fair summary," Kev said.

"Four catastrophic failures in a row," Jeb said. "And he's immortal, so he can't even rage-quit."

"That is the specific problem, yes."

Jeb looked at the yard. Something small and purposeful was moving along the fence line. Neither of them acknowledged it directly.

"You know what gets me?" Jeb said. "The void part. I understand the war and the Movies. Those are at least, you're doing something. But the void. Just sitting there in infinite nothing, waiting for it to feel like peace, and it never does."

"Because AWARENESS generates," Kev said. "That's what it does. Sitting in the void is like asking a fire not to be warm. You can do it. It just won't help."

"I tried it once," Jeb said. "The void thing. Back in, well, back in a cycle we don't need to specify. Lasted about forty minutes before I started involuntarily imagining a sandwich."

"What kind of sandwich?"

"That's not the point, Kev."

"It's a little bit the point."

"Reuben," Jeb admitted. "With the good mustard."

Kev nodded.

A long quiet. The fence-line creature did its fence-line thing. Neither of them looked at it directly.

"This is enough," Jeb said.

"Yeah."

Inside the house, something shifted. The quality of attention behind the screen door, where Mae had been doing something in the kitchen for the last twenty minutes. Neither Kev nor Jeb acknowledged this.

"So Junior's going to go back to the dream," Jeb said. "But this time he's going to find something he wasn't looking for."

"A boy," Kev said. "In a bright house. With a mother who loved him and a world that was, for a little while, exactly the right size."

Jeb picked up the warm Fresca and drank it anyway. "Tell me about the boy."

From inside the house, very quietly, barely a comment at all: "It's always a boy."

They pretended not to hear this. Mae pretended not to have said it. The afternoon continued.

PART TWO

Chapter Six: The Bright Time

The following took place approximately one hundred years before the porch, the cold coffee, and the glimmering yard, in New Orleans, in 1882. The electricity has not arrived yet on this block, but everyone knows it is coming.

The house on Dauphine Street smelled of three things in the afternoon: coal oil from the lamps that lined the parlor walls, gardenia water that Mad mixed herself in a blue ceramic bowl every morning and distributed among the women, and the accumulated warmth of a building that had absorbed its people into its wood and plaster and heavy curtains.

Ren had been born into this smell. He would, for the rest of his life, find himself ambushed by it in unlikely places: a room in a Memphis boarding house, a hotel corridor in Chicago thirty years on. The ambush was always a sudden complete reinstatement of the body he had had at six years old, standing in the afternoon light of the downstairs hallway.

The house had fourteen rooms and seven women and one woman who was not counted in the seven because she ran it, which was Mad, and one boy who was not counted in anything official because he did not exist in any ledger that the city of New Orleans kept, which was Ren.

He had a room. It was at the back of the second floor, past the linen closet and the small window that looked onto the courtyard where the fig tree grew. The room had been used for storage before Ren arrived and was used for storage again after he left. The cot had a coverlet that had been red once and was now a faded indeterminate color. There was a crate for his things and a hook on the door for his coat. The window was just large enough to sit in if you turned sideways, which Ren did most evenings, watching the courtyard go through its colors as the light changed.

• • •

The afternoons were the best time.

In the mornings the house was sleeping or recovering from sleeping, doors closed, the hallways quiet. The women slept late, deeply, without apology. Ren moved through these mornings finding the kitchen, finding Mad, finding whatever bread or cold sweet potato or leftover rice situation represented breakfast, and then finding somewhere to be that was not in anyone's way.

Mad was always up. She was a large woman who moved efficiently. Her hair was black with one stripe of white at the left temple that she had had since she was thirty. She had been advised at various points in her life that she might soften her edges, and had not, on any occasion, taken it.

She was not Ren's mother. His mother was Celestine, who had the room at the front of the second floor and whose beauty made men say things in the parlor that they probably would not have said in other company. Celestine came from somewhere up the river. She did not talk about it. She had eyes that were dark and had seen more than they chose to report, and she loved Ren in a partial way, with very little left over after survival took its share.

She loved him. Ren knew this as a given, a background condition. He had understood very young that what it required from him was that he not need too much of it at one time. Her love was the bar of light from the curtain gap: real, warm, present, and not to be grasped at or it moved.

He did not grasp at it. He watched it instead.

• • •

Mad taught him to read by proximity and accumulation. She read in the kitchen in the early mornings, whatever had accumulated in the parlor in the previous weeks: a Harper's Monthly, a page from someone's discarded novel, the city paper, a tract on phrenology that she found ridiculous and read aloud with commentary. Ren sat at the table with toast and listened.

He watched her lips move slightly when she hit something difficult, watched her finger move under the lines, and asked questions. She answered them without looking up: first with single words, then with sentences, then explaining something properly while continuing to do something else. By the time he was seven he could read anything she put in front of him, and by eight he had read everything that came through the parlor and developed opinions about which Harper's correspondents could construct an argument.

'You read like someone who's going to be trouble,' Mad told him once, not looking up from her own reading, which was at that moment a lengthy editorial about the merits of municipal electric lighting, which the city of New Orleans was considering and which the editorial considered inevitable.

'Is that bad?' Ren said.

'Depends on who you ask,' Mad said. She turned the page. 'The electric company thinks it's going to be fine for everyone. The gas lamp people think it's going to be a catastrophe. You read something like this, you notice they're both right, just about different things.' She set the editorial down. For the first time that morning she looked at him directly. 'That's what reading does, if you let it. Makes you notice that everyone's right about the part they can see.'

Ren considered this. Outside, in the courtyard, the fig tree was doing something with the early light.

'What about the parts they can't see?' he said.

Mad picked up the editorial again. "That's what you're for," she said, and went back to reading.

• • •

Josephine, who had a room on the third floor and who came from somewhere in the direction of Baton Rouge, taught Ren cards. The real games: the ones with actual stakes, played with actual attention, in which the ability to read a face across a table was as important as the cards in your hand. "You're going to need to know what people want," she told him, setting out the cards, "before they know they want it. That's the whole game. Everything else is arithmetic."

Simone, who was from New Orleans proper and had relatives in the Creole quarter and who smelled always of verbena and who spoke French to herself when she was annoyed and English to everyone else, let Ren sit in her room when she was doing her hair in the evenings before work. She did not talk to him during these sessions. She allowed his presence while she moved through the ritual of preparation, and Ren sat in the chair by the window and watched the courtyard go dark.

Yvette, who had the room next to his and who was the youngest of the women and who had been at the house less than a year and who was still, in certain unguarded moments, visibly uncertain whether she had made the right series of decisions to arrive at this room in this house, was honest with him. Honest in the way of someone who occasionally forgets she is talking to a child.

'Do you ever think about what you want to be?' she asked him once, sitting on the floor of his room while he sat in the window, both of them watching the fig tree as if it might do something interesting.

'I want to know things,' Ren said.

'What kind of things?'

He thought about it. The fig tree held still. 'The kind where once you know them you can't unknow them.'

Yvette was quiet. Then she said: 'That's either going to be very good or very hard.'

'Maybe both,' Ren said.

'Maybe both,' she agreed.

• • •

There was a thing about the house that Ren understood and could not have explained to anyone outside it: it was more honest than most of the city that surrounded it.

The city had a great many arrangements that everyone maintained with considerable effort: who was respectable and who was not, who was seen in which parts of town, what was discussed in which company, what the face of a marriage was supposed to look like from the street versus what it was like inside the walls. Ren moved through these arrangements when he moved through the city, to the market, to the docks when he was allowed, along the streets where the daytime world conducted its daytime business, and he could feel the effort everywhere, the sustained performance of arrangements that required constant maintenance.

The house on Dauphine Street did not perform arrangements; it was what it was, and what it was had been decided a long time ago, and the women in it had made their various negotiations with this fact and were getting on with things.

Ren absorbed this. He would carry it his whole life: a deep discomfort with pretending that things were other than what they were, and a deep patience for the complexity of what they actually were.

He learned this in a brothel in New Orleans in 1882, before the evening began.

• • •

The electricity arrived on their block in the autumn of 1883.

Ren was seven. He had been waiting for the electricity. The gas lamp men came first, going up and down the street to do something to the existing fixtures that Ren watched from the window without being able to determine its purpose. Then men with wire, then men attaching things to the outside walls of the buildings up and down the block. Then, for three days, nothing, during which Mad said that was typical and the thing would either work or it wouldn't and there was no point in standing at the window.

Ren stood at the window.

When it happened it was early evening, the light already going sideways and the street beginning its shift from daytime to nighttime commerce. The lights on the block came on all at once, suddenly and completely, as if they had always been there and had simply been waiting for permission.

The street went gold.

The amber of gas was gone. This light was harder and cleaner and brighter, and it fell on the cobblestones and the storefronts and the people passing and made them all sharp. Ren stood at the window and felt something move through him.

He did not write it down. He was seven and did not yet write things down. But the feeling installed itself: the world could become, without warning, more vivid than the night before.

That night he stood at the window and watched the lit street, until Mad came and told him supper was getting cold, and he went because she said so, but he looked back at the gold street over his shoulder all the way to the kitchen.

• • •

Chapter Seven: Hovering Never Fixes Anything

The Monad had by this point burned itself on the void and on transcendence and on the company of its own generated companions. It found Ren's world by proximity.

It came in low. This was new. It had always approached Movies from altitude, from the overview. The last several times at altitude it had found itself unable to feel anything, and it had developed a working hypothesis that altitude was the problem.

It was not entirely wrong about this.

What it found, coming in low, was the house on Dauphine Street at three in the afternoon on an October day. The light was slant and warm and gold.

It found the courtyard. The fig tree. The specific amber warmth of the afternoon in the kitchen where Mad was reading and a boy was at the table eating something and asking questions.

It did not know, yet, what it had found. It only knew that the quality of this particular afternoon, in this particular courtyard, with this particular combination of coal oil and gardenia and the sound of a woman turning a page and a boy's voice asking about electric lights, was something the library did not contain. The thing itself.

The Monad hovered. It had learned, recently and expensively, not to rearrange things.

The boy looked up from the table. There was nothing to see; the Monad occupied no position in the room's visual field. But he looked up: a slight lift of the chin, a brief stillness.

'Something feels different,' Ren said.

'October,' Mad said, without looking up from her reading.

'Not that,' Ren said.

Mad glanced at him. Then out the window. Then back at her reading. 'House settles in the fall,' she said. 'Gets quieter. You can hear things you couldn't hear in summer.'

Ren considered this. He was seven, and willing to accept October as an explanation for most things. But he filed the feeling under a different heading: the room felt slightly more occupied than the number of people in it accounted for.

The Monad did not know that it had just been noticed. It had no category for this; it had been watching Movies for a very long time, and nothing in a Movie had ever looked up.

• • •

The first crumb was not intended as a crumb.

It was the autumn of 1884. Ren was eight. He was sick, thoroughly. He had a fever that had been present for two days and showed no particular intention of leaving. His mother had looked in on him twice and felt his forehead and gone back to her room. Mad had brought him broth and made him drink it and told him to sleep.

He could not sleep. The fever made the ceiling move. The sounds of the house came through the walls, not the nighttime sounds, it was still early, just the afternoon sounds: voices, footsteps, the particular creak of the third step, the sound of the courtyard gate. He listened to these sounds with a thoroughness that revealed their structure. He could hear, in the footsteps, who they belonged to, and in the voices, what they were feeling in the gaps around the words.

He was not frightened, only lonely.

The light in the room changed.

The light in the corner of the room, near the window where the afternoon sun came in at an angle, shifted slightly. It became briefly warmer.

The loneliness did not go away. But something else arrived alongside it, something without a name. The room felt, for an instant, slightly fuller than its occupants accounted for.

Ren lay in his cot with the ceiling doing its fever-movements and the warmth in the corner of the room, and he felt, for reasons that arrived without explanation, slightly less alone.

He filed this under: sometimes things shift. He did not know that something vast and clumsy had just adjusted a quality of light in a room because it could not bear to leave the room the way it was.

The Monad, floating somewhere in the structure of the Movie, sat with what had just happened.

It did not have a folder for it. It opened several folders and found that none of them applied. It considered the folders it had developed for interventions and found that what had just happened was not, precisely, an intervention. That would have required intent. The Monad had not intended this. It had simply been unable to leave the room alone.

This was new information about the Monad.

It sat with this carefully, without rushing it toward a conclusion.

• • •

Ren grew up by accumulation. Information absorbed from the parlor conversations and the kitchen debates and the things Mad said and the things Josephine demonstrated and the things Simone showed him by not performing anything for him and the things Yvette showed him by being honest.

By ten, he could read a room faster than most adults and preferred not to demonstrate this. By eleven, he had strong opinions about which Harper's writers could construct an argument and was not above arguing with them aloud in the kitchen when Mad was there, because Mad would argue back, and their arguments were among the best parts of his days.

By twelve, he was beginning to understand the particular shape of his situation: he had no official existence, no school record, no surname in any ledger, no path from here to anywhere that the city recognized as a path. He was the house's boy. He did not go to the city's schools or appear in its newspapers. He was real in the way that things are real when the people who love them know they are real and the official record disagrees.

He sat with this. He did not argue with it. He had grown up in a house full of women who had made their negotiations with the gap between what they were and what the official record said they were. The house had taught him that the gap was real but that you did not have to let it be the most important thing.

He was twelve. He had not yet had the Awful Night. The world was still fully colored, still warm, still smelling of coal oil and gardenia and the particular warmth of occupied wood. He did not know the color was going to leave. He had never been without it and could not conceive of its absence.

The Monad, hovering close enough now to feel the quality of the boy's attention, knew something was coming. It could see the structure of the Movie from its position. The approach of the Awful Night arrived as a change in pressure.

It did not intervene. It had learned, expensively, that intervention introduced wrongness into the texture of things: Ren's body detected what had been placed rather than grown, and moved away from it. It stayed close, without condition, and waited.

This was the most difficult thing it had ever done.

• • •

Chapter Eight: The Awful Afternoon

It was not night.

It was a Thursday afternoon in November, the light coming through the upstairs window at the low angle of late autumn. The house was quiet. The women were sleeping or dressing or doing the private things that belong to the afternoon. The coal oil smell, the gardenia underneath it, the warmth of the occupied wood. Everything exactly as it always was.

Ren was coming back from the kitchen with a book. He was twelve, not thinking about anything in particular, moving through a hallway with a book inside the only world he had ever known.

A door opened.

Not one of the women's doors. The door at the end of the hall, the room that belonged to a man Ren had seen downstairs many times. A man who brought hard candies sometimes and set them on the parlor table. The house considered him unremarkable.

A boy came out.

Ren's age. Perhaps a year younger. A boy Ren had never seen before. He was straightening his jacket.

He looked at Ren.

Ren looked at him.

Neither of them said anything. The boy went to the stairs and went down them and was gone, and the door at the end of the hall was closed again.

Ren stood very still.

From below, through the floor, voices came up in fragments. Two women, somewhere near the kitchen. He could not catch the words. The tone was sufficient.

The hallway was exactly the same: the late November light, the book in his hand, the coal oil smell, the gardenia, the warmth of the occupied wood.

Nothing was the same.

He went cold.

He was not frightened, only cold, like a window opened in November.

He was the house pet boy.

He had always been the house pet boy. The house's boy who belonged to everyone and therefore to no one. He had been easy and undemanding and grateful for whatever warmth came.

The house had just disclosed the full dimensions of what that meant.

He did not know if this was true, or whether the voices below meant what he understood them to mean or something else entirely, some arrangement that had nothing to do with him. He was twelve and standing in a hallway with a book and what he knew was this: a boy his own age had come out of that room, and the boy had straightened his jacket with that particular careful deliberateness, and the voices below had said what they had said, and the world had shifted two degrees in a direction it could not shift back from.

He stood in the hallway. The house was still all of the things it had always been and was also this. He did not know how to hold the two together, and the holding was already happening anyway, because holding was what he had always done.

He held it so completely and so still that the tear, which had been forming since the tree and had traveled four millimeters over years of careful traveling without arriving, simply stopped, without falling or receding.

The color began to leave.

• • •

The Monad felt it happen.

From the proximity it had been maintaining across the years since the fever, the Monad felt the cold arrive in Ren as the temperature itself. The boy went still in the hallway. He was reorganizing himself around what the door had just disclosed.

It could not arrange anything that would touch what was happening in Ren. What was happening in Ren was the reckoning of a boy who had always known, somewhere below knowing, that the love available to him was partial, and who had just been shown the shape of the partiality in terms he could not reinterpret.

Reckonings have to be had.

What it felt, in the specific closeness of Ren going cold, was something it had not known it was capable of:

Rage.

Not the galaxy-scale aggression of the early Monadic wars. This was smaller and more precise: the rage of something that cares about one specific boy in one specific hallway and has no capacity to change what is happening to him.

It went nowhere. The Monad held it. The rage was ugly and insufficient and it was what there was.

And then it did the only thing available to it.

A door, a back stair, an alley. The city, larger than this hallway, cold and indifferent and available.

The feeling arrived in Ren without a source or a shape. A certainty, arriving whole:

The back stairs, the alley door. Go now.

He went.

He did not decide to go. He was, in the next moment, moving, the book still in his hand, which he would find in the alley later and not remember carrying. Down the back stairs that made none of the sounds the front stairs made. Through the alley door, which was unlocked. Out into the cold November afternoon, which received him with complete indifference.

He did not go back, not that day and not to the version of the house the hallway had disclosed. He would return, because he was twelve and it was his world and he had nowhere else. But the boy who returned was not the boy who had gone down the back stairs.

The Monad followed him out into the cold. Not close enough to be felt. Ren was in no condition for presences. But close enough to keep the thread.

• • •

Chapter Nine: Pleasantville

The color did not leave all at once.

Detection might have led to intervention. The color left slowly. Each day marginally less saturated than the one before, so that by the time anyone noticed, the original colors were so far back that no one could describe what had been lost.

Ren got on with things. This was, in fact, the thing he did best: he managed the distance between himself and what he felt. He was thirteen, then fourteen, then fifteen. He did his work in the house: the chores Mad assigned, the reading he did because the reading was the one thing that did not require him to feel anything in particular, the card games with Josephine who did not know that his poker face had become a permanent condition.

He was not unhappy, and not performing happiness either, only adequately present to the requirements of each day, responsive to what was in front of him, capable of warmth that the women of the house expected and that he provided without great effort. The warmth was at a careful remove.

The tear was on his face. He did not know it was there.

• • •

There was one particular autumn evening with Josephine that Mad remembered for years, though she never spoke of it.

Ren was fourteen. It was a warm evening that arrived in New Orleans late in the season. Josephine dealt the cards. She had been in the house long enough to have developed a practical philosophy about what men wanted and what they needed, and she had extended this philosophy, without announcement, to include boys who were becoming men and who needed something they did not have words for.

They played three hands. Ren won the first. Josephine won the second deliberately, because she had noticed that Ren played differently when he was behind, more present, slightly less managed.

The third hand was the one.

In the middle of it, Josephine set down a card and looked at Ren across the table and said: "You know you're allowed to want things."

Ren looked at his cards. He arranged them slightly. He was very still for a moment.

"I want to win this hand," he said, which was a joke, which was also true, which was also not what she meant and he knew it.

"Yes you do," she said. "And I mean the other things too."

The hand continued. Ren won it, as she had known he would when he was playing from behind and had to be actually present to do it. He thanked her for the game with the courtesy that was his natural register, and he went upstairs, and Josephine sat with the cards spread on the table before she gathered them.

She had not reached him; she had reached toward him, and he had received the reaching and filed it under something he did not have a label for. The filing was the only thing available to him at fourteen.

Patience ran through her, through the house, through Mad above all things.

The years had a particular quality. Everything in its place, nothing broken, the light coming in at the same angle every afternoon. Ren moved through them competently, keeping the warmth available and the distance managed. The house asked nothing of him he could not provide.

He did not know he was waiting.

• • •

The Monad, across those eleven years, did not leave.

This surprised it. It had not decided to stay; it had simply found, each time it moved to extend its attention elsewhere, that the thread back to Ren was still there. The specific quality of Ren's attention, even at the careful remove, was something it was not finished with.

It had accumulated, across eleven years of proximity, something it did not have a folder for. The closest the library could offer was: investment. The specific interest of something present across years, implicated in the outcome by virtue of the presence.

The Monad stayed and adjusted nothing. It intervened in nothing. It maintained the proximity, which had become, over eleven years, companionship.

But the Monad was also changing. Water changes what it moves through, and is changed by moving through it.

In the beginning, it had stayed because the thread was interesting, because Ren's quality of attention was a thing it had not seen before, and because the dream substance available here was richer than most. This was honest.

Across eleven years, the quality of why it stayed shifted. Less bright with purpose. More quiet.

The Monad was, by the eleventh year, staying for Ren's sake and not its own.

Ren did not know it was there. He felt, some days, a warmth behind the silence that he had no explanation for. He had been feeling it since childhood, since the dust in the bar of light and the shifted quality of October light in the corner of his room, and had filed it under: sometimes things shift, and continued to file it there. He did not know the file was a person.

• • •

Mad watched him. She did not say anything. She was a woman who waited until she was sure what she wanted to say. She waited, patiently, for him to be ready for whatever came next.

Chapter Ten: What Came Through the Raccoon

The second crumb arrived in the winter of 1896, when Ren was twenty.

He had left the house on Dauphine Street the previous year, because Mad had looked at him one morning across the kitchen table with the directness of a woman who has been waiting a long time to say something and has decided the waiting is over, and had said: 'You're going to go now. Not because you have to. Because staying is going to keep you in the shape the staying made you.'

He had gone, and found work on the docks, then in a printing house, then as a reader for an elderly man who could no longer see well enough to read his own correspondence and who paid Ren in room and board and the occasional opinion delivered with more confidence than the situation warranted. He was living in a rooming house near the river when the winter came in hard off the water.

He was at a breaking point. Not the dramatic kind. Ren did not have dramatic breaking points. The quiet kind: he had been fine for so long that being fine had become its own exhaustion, and he could feel the weight of it in his body, a depletion of the resources fine-ness costs.

He went out, not with a destination, just out, because the room had become the wrong size. The streets were cold and mostly empty, the river making its river sounds somewhere to the left, the gas lamps doing their amber work on the wet cobblestones. He walked without direction.

He found the ditch by nearly falling into it.

The ditch was at the edge of a lot near the river, one of the indeterminate spaces that cities produce between their intentions, just a space where mud and water and the detritus of the adjacent buildings accumulated. In the ditch was a raccoon.

It had a crooked front leg.

Ren stood at the edge of the ditch and looked at the raccoon and the raccoon looked back at him: focused, comprehensive, without apparent alarm. It had decided to cooperate with its own survival.

He did not think about whether to lift it. He lifted it. The weight was specific and complete and warm against his chest, and his arms discovered, in real time, that they knew how to hold this thing.

The raccoon conducted its rapid assessment. The situation was: acceptable. It settled.

And something happened.

What shifted was the texture of the night, and what arrived was a feeling, specific and warm and without explanation:

that he was not as alone as the room had been insisting. There was something in the texture of being alive that he had been refusing to receive.

He stood in the cold with the raccoon against his chest and felt, for the first time since the hallway, company that did not ask anything of him. Not the cold of indifference. Closer to hunger.

He did not know that the Monad, which had been maintaining its proximity across seven years of the rooming house and the printing house and the docks and the long depletion of the washed-out years, had aimed. Had looked at the structure of the night and found the raccoon and done, with considerable care and no guarantee of success, the only thing it could do without introducing wrongness: arranged nothing. Been close, when Ren lifted the raccoon, so what came through the raccoon's weight was not only the raccoon's weight.

The Monad had not sent the raccoon; it had sent itself, by being a raccoon, in the world, doing raccoon things. It had been there, and its presence had colored the moment.

What came through the raccoon was real. Ren could not have said what it was. He would later describe it to Jeb on the porch as the warmth behind the silence.

He carried the raccoon to the edge of the lot, where the ground was dry. He set it down. It conducted another assessment. It shook once. It looked at him for one more moment. Then it moved off into the dark.

He watched it go.

There was a tear on his face. He did not know it was there. It had traveled further than it ever had before, below his cheekbone now, trembling with the cold and the weight of the raccoon. It did not fall. He was still holding things. But it was closer.

He walked back to the rooming house through the cold streets, and the room was the right size when he returned to it, and he slept.

• • •

Chapter Eleven: What the Warmth Was Made Of

It was some years later, with Ren in his late twenties, living in a different city, working as a typesetter for a man named Duchamp who had strong opinions about leading and kerning and the moral dimensions of justified text, that he began to understand something about the warmth.

He had been practicing into it for years, taking the feeling from the ditch, from the raccoon, from the quality of company that asked nothing of him, and building a practice around it. There was no teacher, only the feeling itself, which he used as the curriculum.

He practiced into the warmth.

And the warmth was there. He was not imagining it. On the mornings when the practice was clean, when he had managed to be simply present to whatever was present, the warmth was reliably, undeniably there. Available. Real in the way that the coal oil smell had been real.

What he had not understood was that it had faces.

This arrived slowly. He was in the printshop one afternoon, setting type with focused attention, when something in the quality of the warmth shifted, became, briefly, specific in a way it usually was not. As if the warmth had, for a moment, a face.

The face was Mad's.

Not a vision. He was not having visions; he was setting type in a printshop in an ordinary afternoon. But the quality of it: the particular warmth that had no patience for pretending things were other than they were. That warmth, which had taught him to read, had told him he was going to be trouble, had sent him out into the world.

He set the type very carefully and did not move for a moment.

Then, across the next weeks, the others arrived in the same way: briefly, specifically, as qualities of warmth rather than presences. Josephine's warmth, which had taught him cards and expected him to use what he learned. Simone's warmth, which had been being allowed to be in a room without having to be anything in particular. Yvette's warmth, which had treated him as someone who could handle what he was being told.

And his mother's warmth, the hardest of all to receive, because it was real and insufficient at once, and receiving it required holding both.

He held both.

The warmth behind the silence was not impersonal. It had never been impersonal. It was the aggregate warmth of every person who had ever received something from him.

Of every woman in the house who had been kind to him. Of the reader he had read aloud to, who had died the previous year, who had said once that Ren's voice reading made the words come from somewhere other than the page. Of Duchamp, who would not have said he loved Ren but who had given him the good machines to work on.

It was the warmth of Junior, which Ren filed under: something larger, present, somewhat clumsy, occasionally well-intentioned in ways that didn't land. A presence that needed something from him that it couldn't name, and that he was, without knowing it, providing simply by being what he was.

The abandoned boy was not abandoned. He had never been abandoned; he had been unable to see the full shape of what surrounded him because he had been looking for the shape of what was missing. The looking had been a form of accuracy: the love had been partial, the absence had been real, the gap had been there and was not to be denied.

But the accounting had been wrong.

He stood at the type case in Duchamp's printshop and he did the addition and the world got slightly more vivid. Not the electric-light revelation of 1883. A small unmistakable increment. A degree of color that had not been there that morning. The specific amber of the afternoon light on the metal type. The smell of the ink, suddenly present again after he had stopped smelling it for months.

He picked up the composing stick and went back to work.

He would be adding for years.

• • •

There came a morning, Ren in his mid-thirties now, living in the city that would eventually be the city where Jeb and Kev sat on the porch with their cold coffee, when the warmth had a wrong note in it.

Not wrong in the sense of bad. Colored. Something with its own quality, its own particular need, its own agenda, however clumsy.

He had been practicing into the warmth long enough that he could feel the difference between the warmth and the warmth-plus-something. He did not know what the something was. He knew that something in the channel wanted something from him.

He had recognized this quality his whole life. Every woman in the house had needed something from him: his compliance, his ease, his unobtrusiveness, his convenience. He had given all of these things, with genuine warmth and without resentment, mostly, because they were what was available to give.

But he was thirty-five now, and the giving had a different texture. He could feel, in the warmth behind the silence, the shape of a need he had been meeting without knowing he was meeting it. Something vast and very young, old in years but inexperienced in being, that needed him to be present so it could be in proximity to presence without knowing how to be present itself.

He was being useful. He recognized the shape of it.

He sat with this and didn't feel betrayed. He had been useful in every relationship he had ever had: to the house, to the women, to the reader who needed his voice, to Duchamp who needed his accuracy. Being useful was the thing he was best at, the thing that had allowed him to make his way in the world with no official existence and no surname in any ledger.

But he was thirty-five, and he had just done the accounting in Duchamp's printshop, and the accounting had changed things. And the changed accounting required, at some point, a changed practice. He could not keep practicing into a warmth that was colored by someone else's need without the practice itself becoming a service to someone else's need rather than a genuine arrival at his own ground.

He simply stopped reaching toward the warmth. There was no one to tell.

He stopped reaching toward the warmth and started simply being present, like the raccoon in the yard, like the fig tree in the courtyard: without the slight transactional quality of a practice still oriented toward getting something.

He just sat.

With the morning and the coffee, with the quality of the day, without asking it to also be warm.

The Monad felt the withdrawal as the loss of contact when someone you have been steadily reaching toward stops reaching back. Not a loss of the person. Ren was still there, still entirely himself. But the transaction had ended, and a particular quality of access went with it.

It could not follow where Ren had gone. Where Ren had gone was accessible only by arriving, which required stopping the careful proximity that was close enough to feel the warmth without being changed by it.

The Monad sat with this for what it would later describe to no one in particular as a very long time.

Then it did the only thing left. It stopped reaching and hovering. It let the distance close, not through effort, not through intention, not through any of the capacities it had been relying on. It simply allowed itself to be where Ren was in the same way that Ren had allowed himself to be where the morning was.

It arrived.

It arrived as itself, present, in this morning, with the coffee and the quality of the day.

Neither of them knew what had happened. Both felt that something had changed in the structure of things.

• • •

He lived a long life. Long in years and long in the other thing, harder to measure, which is the degree to which a life has accumulated itself rather than merely accumulated time.

He never talked about the house on Dauphine Street. Not because he was ashamed of it, Ren was not, in the end, a man who spent much energy on shame, having grown up in a place that had made a working peace with the gap between what it was and what the official record said it was. But because the house was not a story he knew how to tell so that it would land correctly, and he had learned from Mad that precision mattered: you said the thing when you knew how to say the thing, and until then you let it be inside you, doing its work.

It did its work. The women and the coal oil smell and Mad's directness and the afternoons in Simone's chair and the cards with Josephine and Yvette's honest questions and his mother's love given in the only portions available, all of it was load-bearing in the structure of what he became. Because of the house.

He had taken this with him everywhere and let it be the grain of the wood.

He had never quite learned to ask for more than was being offered. This remained true into his old age, and it was the thing that Jeb, who knew him better than most people ever knew anyone, could feel as a gap in the conversation sometimes: the careful calibration of wanting that had been installed in a boy on a mattress in a back room. The calibration had been loosening for years. It was still there.

But he had done the accounting. He knew what surrounded him. The sum was not nothing; it was, in fact, staggering, if you stood still long enough to add it.

He stood still and added.

The world got its color back. Not all at once. It came back the way it had left, gradually, each day a degree more saturated than the one before, until one morning the amber of the printshop and the fig tree in the courtyard and the gold of the electric street and Mad's stripe of white and the specific weight of a raccoon deciding the situation was acceptable were all vivid again.

The tear was on his face.

It had been traveling for decades. It was very nearly at his chin.

In a field, in late afternoon light, in a city one hundred years from where he started, it was going to fall.

But not yet. First there were the years between. The evenings with the coffee that was always almost the right temperature. The porch, and the cold coffee, and whatever was moving in the strange light near the fence, and a raccoon working the fence line.

He had a lot to learn from the raccoon.

The raccoon was patient.

It had nothing but time.

★ *The Phone: Disconnected*

The fluorescent light above Marvin's pod buzzed. The blinds along the east wall were drawn. The screen in front of Marvin showed the next number on the call list and the script that went with it.

Marvin picked up the headset. He fitted it over his ear.

His mug sat at the corner of the desk. The mug said WORLD'S OKAYEST DAD in white letters on a navy background. There was a chip on the rim.

Marvin reached for the mug. His thumb found the chip.

March, and she was twelve. She called in the middle of shift. I don't remember what about.

He lifted the mug, took a sip, and set it back down.

In the drawer beside his keyboard there was a postcard from a woman in Indianapolis named Janelle Park. Not the Janelle in the next pod. A customer Janelle, who had sent the postcard in 2007 after Marvin had spent forty minutes on the phone with her not selling her the satellite TV package she had called about because she was crying about her mother. The postcard said: "You were kind. I won't forget." Marvin had read it twice that day. He read it again now. He put it back in the drawer.

He dialed the next number on the screen.

The system on his end registered a failure to connect. It beeped once. It advanced to the next prompt.

Something happened in his chest.

Marvin's hand went to the desk and stayed there. His other hand was still on the mug. The headset was on his ear.

The thing in his chest finished.

Marvin's hand on the mug let go. The mug stayed where it was. The headset slid off his ear and onto his shoulder.

Across the call center floor, Janelle in the next pod looked over. She said his name. He did not answer. She stood up, crossed to his pod, put a hand on his shoulder, and said his name again.

Other people came over. Someone called 911. Janelle held Marvin's hand.

The mug sat on the desk with a chip on the rim.

• • •

Marvin was standing somewhere. He was not at his desk. The floor under his feet was not the call center floor.

He was holding the headset.

He looked at the headset, then up.

There was a man standing in front of him. The man was not in a hurry; he was just looking at Marvin.

I don't have a script for this.

The man said nothing.

"I think I'm dead," Marvin said.

"Yes," the man said.

"Oh," Marvin said.

He set the headset down. The headset stayed where he set it.

"Where am I?"

"With me."

"Are you God?"

"No."

"Are you somebody who knows God?"

"No."

"Okay," Marvin said.

He looked around.

"Are you a customer?"

The man laughed.

"No, Marvin. I am not a customer."

"You know my name."

"Yes."

The man did not speak. He looked at Marvin, who looked back.

"You may stay," the man said. "If you want to."

"Do I have somewhere else to be?"

"No."

"Then I guess I'll stay."

The man nodded.

Marvin picked up the headset. He held it. He did not put it on.

"It is good that you are here," the man said.

Marvin nodded.

Marvin Finkelworth stood next to a man he had just met.

He stayed standing.

★ *The Porch: Something Leaks Through*

Kev had stopped talking. Something had landed.

Jeb waited.

Out in the yard, something small had moved at the edge of the grass and then hadn't. The Diet Fresca on the railing had gone flat.

"The thing about the boy," Kev said finally, "is that he never tried to be more than he was. He was just a boy in a house, with a mother and a raccoon. And when the presence came, the thing that was not the house, he didn't try to understand it or master it or become it. He just let it be there."

"And that's what Junior couldn't do," Jeb said.

"Couldn't, wouldn't, didn't know how. Take your pick." Kev adjusted his glasses. "Junior is a Monad. He's vast and powerful and contains multitudes, like the man said. And none of that prepared him for a boy who was warm without trying."

"Because warmth isn't a power," Jeb said.

"No. It's a quality. And you can't achieve a quality. You can only have one."

Something moved in the yard again. This time Jeb thought he caught the specific shape: low, unhurried. Gone before he could confirm.

"Now," Kev said, "now Junior goes looking for the boy. And this is where it gets interesting. Because Junior thinks he's the teacher."

"Oh no," Jeb said, but he was smiling.

"Oh yes," Kev said.

And somewhere, not on the porch, not in the yard, not in any geography that shared a border with Diet Fresca, Ren looked up from what he was doing.

He had been reading. The fig tree was holding still. For a moment, less than a moment, he heard something. Not with his ears.

Two voices, men. Talking about him with a familiarity that should have been alarming and wasn't. One of them had said something about warmth not being a power, and the other had agreed, and there was a sound underneath it that

Ren could not identify but that felt like wood and afternoon and something carbonated.

Then it was gone.

Ren went back to his reading. He left a small part of his attention on the place where the voices had been.

PART THREE

The Monad, Before It Knew Better

Chapter Twelve: When You Are the Only One

(Why would any being, vast or small, want a porch?)

The Monad sat in his field. He had run every interior scenario, expanded his boundary, run more, expanded again. There was nothing in his field he had not put there.

He stayed in his field.

After a while he generated a companion.

The companion stood in front of him and looked at him. The Monad looked back.

"Hello," the Monad said.

"Hello," the companion said.

The Monad put a question to the companion, which gave an answer.

The Monad generated a second companion. Then a third.

The three companions stood in front of him. They had conversations with him and with each other.

The Monad gave one of them the quality of pushing back. He labeled this one sharp, and it produced counterarguments. The Monad answered them.

Eventually the sharp companion agreed with the Monad.

The Monad ran this sequence many times. Different qualities, different disagreements. They all agreed with him in the end.

They are very good companions. They agree with me even when I have set them up to disagree.

The aloneness is still here.

He let the companions uncurl. He generated new ones. They agreed with him.

Still here.

• • •

He was in his field, having just completed a proof establishing that Experience Requires an Experiencer and Therefore Only One Valid Experiencer Can Logically Exist. He held the completed proof. He moved to file it.

A garbage can appeared in his field.

The Monad looked at the garbage can. The garbage can was dented. Its lid was slightly ajar.

Inside the can, through the ajar lid, the Monad could see a crumpled paper. The crumpled paper was the proof he had just completed.

A raccoon appeared in his field.

The raccoon walked up to the garbage can and knocked it over. The lid came off, and the raccoon put its head into the can. The raccoon located something inside the can and pulled it out with its teeth. The thing was edible; it ate half in one bite, and the other half hung from its mouth.

The raccoon did not look at the Monad.

The raccoon turned and left the field, the other half of the morsel still hanging from its mouth.

The garbage can stayed where it had fallen. The proof stayed inside.

The Monad looked at the garbage can.

That came from outside.

My library does not have a raccoon in it.

The raccoon did not ask permission to be in my field.

It did not look at me.

• • •

He extended his field-wall outward.

He kept extending it.

He extended it further.

The field-wall met something.

He held the contact.

This is not POTENTIALITY.

The thing on the other side pushed.

The Monad pushed back.

Chapter Thirteen: Party Crasher, Monad Style

The Monad turned his attention toward the Movies. He looked at one. He brought his attention down toward the surface of the Movie.

He held just outside the surface and looked.

The Movie was a small world: streets, buildings, weather that held between rain and the suggestion of rain and stayed there.

Inside one of the buildings, in one of the rooms, on a mattress on a floor, there was a child.

The Monad looked at the child.

This is the pattern. Child, neglect, silence.

He held the child in his attention. He waited for the pattern to play out.

The child did something else.

The child was looking at a bar of light coming through a gap in the curtain. There were dust motes in the bar of light. The dust motes rose and fell in the slow drift of a room that had not been opened to outside air in some time.

The child looked at the dust. He kept looking. He did not look away.

He is not waiting for something better.

The Monad watched the child watching the dust.

This is not in the folder.

He brought his attention closer to the child.

• • •

The child's name was Ren. He was five years old.

The Monad watched Ren over the next several years of Movie-time. Ren grew and became a person who could attend to things.

The Monad watched Ren attend to things.

He is doing what I have not yet learned how to do. I came down here because I want what he has.

The Monad continued to watch Ren. He stayed close enough to feel the quality of Ren's attention, but above body, above weather. He did not enter the cold or the hunger.

• • •

One night Ren left his room.

Ren walked out of the building. He was barefoot. The ground outside was cold. He walked to a tree, stood by it, and held his breath.

A tear formed at the inner corner of his left eye. The tear traveled four millimeters and stopped on his cheekbone. It did not fall.

Ren stood by the tree with the tear on his cheekbone.

Ren breathed out.

Something moved from Ren toward the Monad.

The Monad held very still.

Something arrived at the Monad that the Monad had not generated.

The Monad held the contact.

Contact.

The cold of the night was around Ren and around the Monad.

The Monad held the contact until Ren went back inside.

Ren went back inside. The Monad stayed in the dark.

That came from him. He did not know he was sending it.

I did not generate this.

• • •

The Monad continued watching Ren.

When Ren was fifteen he sat with a book, read it, and closed it.

The Monad felt the closing of the book.

The Monad pushed warmth toward Ren. He did not use language.

Ren sat very still, then looked up. He held still for another moment. Then he put the book on a high shelf and stood up.

Ren went to find something to do with his hands.

The Monad held in the place where Ren had been sitting.

He felt it as pressure. I had interrupted what he was sitting with.

Three years passed in Movie-time. Ren took the book down from the high shelf, read it, and stayed with it.

The Monad watched.

• • •

When Ren was in his mid-twenties he was on the steps outside the building where he worked. He had food in a paper bag beside him.

The light came between two buildings and hit the brick wall across from where Ren was sitting. The wall was the color of amber.

Ren looked up at the wall.

The Monad watched Ren look at the wall.

If I lean forward now, I can show him what this means.

The Monad leaned forward. He sent an offer toward Ren.

Ren put the paper bag down on the step beside him. He looked at the wall for another moment, then looked away, stood up, and went back inside the building. He did not look at the wall again that evening.

The Monad held in the place where Ren had been sitting. The amber light continued on the brick wall.

He felt me reach. He closed the door.

I offered help. I took the moment from him, and have been doing this his whole life.

The Monad pulled back.

He stayed where he was.

Chapter Fourteen: Archimedes Pays a Call

Archimedes is old. He has been through the burning, the void and its lack of satisfied customers, the Movies entered wrong, the war with another Monad, and the long patient discovery that the particular is the entire point. He arrived at Aplomb in a previous Maha cycle.

He has, across his education, developed a sincere love of the Movies, as a genuine appreciator of the form. Archimedes has favorites. He is not embarrassed about this. A Monad that has finally understood what the particular is worth is not going to pretend that certain particulars are not more magnificent than others.

He had been watching Junior for some time. Not obsessively. He kept a peripheral eye on it.

He had also watched Junior make the three mistakes with Ren, and had made a firm private decision to do nothing about it yet. Junior had not finished suffering, which was the work. An elder who interrupted the work because the watching was uncomfortable was an elder serving his own discomfort rather than the student's education, and Archimedes had made that mistake once, in an earlier cycle, and did not make it twice.

But Junior had now made the mistakes. Had made them completely and thoroughly. Junior was, in Archimedes's assessment, at maximum suffering.

He pinged next to Junior's field. Not inside: no Monad enters another Monad's field, any more than you enter a stranger's chest cavity uninvited. Outside, just adjacent. Close enough that Junior would register the presence, which Junior did immediately, with alarm. Junior had very recently been through a war.

This outside was not trouble. It had, in the space between one moment and the next, arranged itself into a small round table with two chairs, a white tablecloth, a teapot, and two cups already poured, steaming.

In one of the chairs: a figure who had chosen, for this visit, the form of a late-Victorian English naturalist. Tweed. The expression of a man who has catalogued seventeen thousand species of beetle and found each one genuinely interesting.

He gestured at the empty chair. He waited for Junior to assume a reasonable form. This took a while. Junior's forms, at this stage of its development, tended toward the grandiose: vast geometries, impossible light, the visual vocabulary of a being that has not yet learned that true power does not need to announce itself.

Junior arrived eventually at something vaguely humanoid and sat down, which was the correct answer even if the form was still somewhat larger than the chair strictly required.

"Excellent," said Archimedes. He poured. "I am Archimedes. You are Junior. Drink your tea."

Junior, who had a great many urgent things to say about its recent experiences and had been composing them into a suitably impressive account for some time, found that it had instead picked up the teacup. The tea was, against all reasonable expectation, excellent.

"You have been having a difficult time," Archimedes said. It was a description of observed conditions, offered without judgment.

Junior began to explain. The war, the void. The Movies and their refusal to provide what they had clearly been designed to provide. The three mistakes with Ren. The outline of its proof, now unfortunately in a garbage can somewhere, which had been genuinely excellent and deserved better than the editorial treatment it had received from an unsolicited raccoon.

Archimedes listened to all of this with complete attention. Junior, who had been running shadow-companions for company and had therefore not been genuinely listened to since before the concept of listening existed, felt something happen in the region where its field wall was thinnest.

When Junior had finished, Archimedes was quiet for a moment.

"Yes," he said finally. "That is more or less how it goes."

Junior waited for more. There was no more.

"You are going to tell me what I'm doing wrong," Junior said.

"No," said Archimedes. "You are going to discover what you're doing wrong. I'm going to have tea."

He poured himself another cup. The teapot had not diminished. Junior stared at it. The staring had the quality of a being that is beginning to suspect that the problem may not be external.

"You enjoy the Movies," Archimedes said, as the beginning of something. "Or you are trying to. I have found, personally, that the enjoyment improves considerably once one stops approaching them as a problem to be solved." He settled back in his chair. "At present I am particularly taken with a young woman in a Movie some distance from here. Remarkable presence. She disappears entirely into a role, not in the sense of losing herself, but in the sense of being so completely herself within the role that the distinction becomes irrelevant. I find it," he paused, "instructive."

Junior considered this. It had, it realized, a position on the Movies that it had not previously articulated even to itself.

There was a performer it kept returning to. Had kept returning to across its tourist visits: a man in Ren's Movie's era who appeared in various productions wearing an expression of such profound smoldering significance that lesser beings simply wept at the weight of it. He had a quality that Junior had filed, with some admiration, under: gravitas of the highest order, possibly cosmic in origin.

"There is a performer," Junior said, with some reverence, "called Mike Myers."

Archimedes received this with complete stillness. He looked at Junior with the warm and genuinely delighted recognition of an elder Monad who has just learned exactly where a younger one currently is in its education.

"He plays a large Scottish man," Junior continued, with the tone of one building an airtight case, "who wants things with his entire being, at tremendous volume, and knows that he wants them and cannot stop wanting them, and is simultaneously appalled by himself for the wanting and completely committed to the wanting, and all of this happens at the same time, with remarkable transparency and no apparent embarrassment. And then he also plays an evil man who builds a lair and holds the world hostage and requires a very particular chair and has a son he is simultaneously disappointed in and devoted to, and the evil is so committed, so thoroughly performed, that it becomes its own kind of illuminating, because what the evil man actually is, underneath the plan for world domination, is someone who very urgently needs to be taken seriously and has not yet found a more efficient method."

Junior paused. "I find both characters extremely instructive," it said, with a dignity that was not entirely aware of itself.

"Yes," said Archimedes. "Quite." He picked up his teacup. Set it down. Picked it up again. "He understood something, that performer. Both characters are the same philosophical problem approached from different directions. One wants everything and is transparent about it. One performs significance and believes the performance. The interesting thing is that he plays both with complete sympathy. He does not mock them. He loves them. Which means," Archimedes said, "that he understood them from the inside. Which is the only place understanding of that quality ever originates."

Junior filed this under: unexpectedly not embarrassing. Then filed it under: possibly the most useful thing anyone has said to me about my own situation.

"The large Scottish man," Archimedes said, "is instructive in a different way than you think. Not because the wanting is funny. Because the wanting is honest. It is the most honest performance of wanting that has been committed to film in that era. And honesty about wanting, even tremendous loud Scottish wanting, is the beginning of the particular. You cannot be in the particular if you are pretending you don't want things. The particular is made of wanting things. The question is only whether you can want them without requiring them to be different than they are."

Somewhere at the edges of Junior's attention there was a signal. A room. A name it did not yet have a folder for. It filed this under: later.

"You have found someone," Archimedes said, without looking up from his tea. It was not a question.

"She named me," Junior said. The sentence arrived with weight.

"Yes," said Archimedes. "They often do. The ones who name things tend to be the ones worth watching." He set down his cup. "You cannot use her. You know that. Not because it would harm her. Because using her would prevent you from receiving what she actually has to offer."

Junior thought about this. The peripheral warmth it had registered was still there, at the edge of its attention.

"What do I do now," Junior said. The question had none of its previous grandiosity. It was simply a question: small, sincere, the question of a being that has exhausted its own answers and is, for perhaps the first time, genuinely asking.

Archimedes looked out at a middle distance. "There is a boy," he said. "You have been watching him. You have been watching him incorrectly, but you have been watching him, which is something. Go back. Watch him correctly this time."

"How do I watch him correctly?"

"The way you just watched Mae," Archimedes said. "Without wanting anything from it. Without a folder ready."

Junior sat with this. In the salon, Darlene's dryer chimed. She emerged from under it with the slightly dazed expression of someone returning from a particularly vigorous interior world, patted her hair experimentally, and declared it excellent. Mae agreed that it was excellent.

Archimedes stood. "You are going to be fine," he said. "Not immediately. Not without additional difficulty, which I am afraid I cannot spare you and would not if I could. But fine. Eventually."

He straightened his jacket. Then he looked at Junior.

"The raccoon," he said, "is coming."

Junior looked at the empty chair. On the table: the teapot, the two cups, the tablecloth. Then looked back to where Archimedes had been, which was now simply: the space next to its field wall.

The teacup was still warm. Junior held it.

Chapter Fifteen: Sovereign and Soft

The Monad had been watching Ren fail at the same thing for eleven years and had not known what to call the failure.

It could describe the symptom. Ren moved through his days carefully. The warmth real but held at remove. The presence genuine but managed. The attention he brought to the physical world, the grain of wood, the weight of a tool in the hand, the specific amber of evening light on brick, was full and honest; the attention he brought to people was slightly less full, slightly more curated.

The Monad had filed this under: adaptive suppression, sustained, possibly permanent. It had watched something it was only beginning to recognize as suffering rather than as information.

What it had not understood, what it did not have the vocabulary for, because the vocabulary had not yet arrived at the proximity where Junior was hovering, was the nature of the membrane itself. Not what Ren was doing. What Ren was *made of*, in the moments when the world came toward him and he received it. The texture of the surface: how hard or soft it was, whether things landed or bounced.

The word arrived, as words tend to arrive, from somewhere unexpected.

• • •

Archimedes was watching a different Movie at the time. Old Monads maintain multiple attentions: separate threads present simultaneously, none diminished by the others. He was watching a porch. Two men. Cold coffee and stars and the steady hum of a long ongoing exchange.

The taller of the two men, the one with the philosophical turn of mind, the one who had been working on something for years and was nearly through to the other side of it, said something that stopped Archimedes in the act of reaching for his own tea.

"So when I'm brittle," the man said, "the world feels brittle. When I'm gooey… stuff lines up. People soften."

Archimedes set his tea down.

He had heard a great many formulations of this insight across a great many cycles, in a great many traditions and vocabularies, stated by people who had arrived at it through decades of formal practice and by people who had arrived at it through the curriculum of having their lives taken apart, and had filed seventeen thousand variations on the theme.

But *gooey*.

He had not had gooey.

He pinged Junior.

• • •

Junior arrived at the now-familiar adjacency to Archimedes's field. Less enormous than before, still slightly more than necessary, heading in the right direction.

"There's a concept," Archimedes said, without preamble. He had found, with Junior, that preamble was counterproductive. Junior was a Monad that appreciated directness. It had been burned enough by indirection, by the gap between what it expected and what it received, that a certain plainness had become one of the things it valued most. Archimedes respected this. "I want you to sit with it. Not analyze it. Sit with it."

"I can do that," Junior said, with the specific confidence of something that is committed to attempting it.

"Two states," Archimedes said. "Brittle. And gooey."

He waited. Not for Junior to respond, he knew Junior would respond, Junior always responded, but for the words to arrive rather than the response. There was a difference, and the difference was the entire lesson, and he had learned long ago not to shorten the interval in which it could happen.

Junior was quiet. This was already notable.

"Brittle," Archimedes said, "is what happens when a being organizes itself around protection. It decides, at some level below the level of decision, that the world is primarily something to be managed. To be received at a controlled distance. It develops a competent surface, often warm, even. It can perform warmth with considerable skill. But the warmth is at a remove, because the surface has to maintain its integrity, and genuine warmth, the kind that allows the other to actually land, requires softening the surface, and softening the surface is the one thing the surface cannot do without ceasing to be a surface."

Another pause.

"So everything bounces," Junior said. Not a question.

"Everything bounces," Archimedes confirmed. "The world comes toward the brittle being and reflects off it. Not because the world is hostile. Because the surface cannot receive. The synchronicities are there. They are always there, the Movie is always speaking in its particular language of resonance and echo and the small meaningful accidents that the symbolic layer generates when it has something to say, but the brittle being cannot hear them over the sound of its own management. It is too busy maintaining the surface to notice what the surface is preventing from arriving."

Junior was quiet again. Archimedes watched something happen in the quality of Junior's attention that he had been waiting several Maha cycles to see: it stopped being the attention of something assessing information and became the attention of something recognizing itself. The difference was subtle and total.

"Gooey," Archimedes said.

"Yes," Junior said. Just that.

"Gooey is not the absence of self. This is important. Gooey is not dissolution. A being that has become gooey has not lost itself in the world. It is not permeable to the point of having no shape, no character, nothing distinguishing it from the field around it. The raccoon on the fence is not dissolved into the fence; it is entirely itself, more completely so than anything else in the immediate vicinity." He paused. "And the raccoon is soft."

Junior said nothing. This was the correct response.

"Sovereign and soft," Archimedes said. "Both. Simultaneously. Fully itself and fully open. Not defending the self because the self is not in danger. The self was never in danger from contact, only from the belief that contact would damage it."

The familiar logic of the trap. Junior had been in this trap and recognized the shape of it from the inside: everything slightly smaller and more two-dimensional than you remember, and exactly right.

"He has a surface," Junior said. Not about Archimedes. Both of them knew who the he was.

"He built it young," Archimedes said, without judgment. "From good materials. It has served him. It got him to here, which is not nowhere. The surface did its job and does not know that job is done; surfaces are not good at knowing when their work is finished."

"How does it come down?"

Archimedes picked up his tea, set it down, and looked at Junior.

"It doesn't come down," he said. "That's not the right frame. You cannot dismantle a surface by attacking it. The surface will defend itself against dismantling with everything it has, which is considerable, and the attempt to take it apart will only make it harder. This has been tried."

"Then how."

"Something has to land," Archimedes said. "Something that arrives so completely without threat, with such total absence of agenda, that the surface has nothing to defend against. Something that is so entirely itself, so gooey in its own nature, that proximity to it makes the hardness feel, not wrong. Not something to be ashamed of. Just: unnecessary. Heavy. Like armor in a room where there is no war."

They were both quiet. The Movie with the porch continued in its peripheral way. The two men on the porch had moved on to something else, one of them was laughing at something, the specific laugh of a person who has recently discovered that their own suffering is funny, which is one of the better laughs available to human beings and one of the ones that tends to arrive late in the education.

"The raccoon," Junior said.

"Yes," said Archimedes.

"But that's. It doesn't try. The raccoon doesn't try to help him."

"Correct."

"It doesn't know it's helping."

"Also correct."

"So how does it—" Junior stopped. Something shifted in the quality of its attention again. "Oh," it said.

"Yes," said Archimedes.

"It's not doing anything. It's just being gooey. Completely. In the same space. And the contrast—"

"Is information," Archimedes said. "Not as a lesson or as guidance. Simply present. The raccoon is entirely itself, entirely soft, entirely without a surface, and when you are in proximity to something like that, you feel the weight of your own armor in a way you cannot feel it when everything around you is also armored. The contrast does not argue; it simply is. And the being with the surface, if the being with the surface is the kind of being who pays attention, and Ren pays attention, Ren has always paid attention, it is the one thing that was never lost. The being with the surface notices."

"And then?"

"And then," Archimedes said, "it's his. Not given, not taught. His. Which is the only way it works. A softness that comes from outside is still a transaction. It's still something arriving with an agenda, the agenda of helping, and the surface will feel the agenda and brace against it, because agendas are threats, even kind ones, even loving ones, even the most well-intentioned ones." He looked at Junior with the affection of someone who is also, in some way, talking about Junior's own history. "Which is something you already know."

Junior was quiet.

"You pushed," Junior said finally. "I pushed. In the amber light. I leaned toward him with everything I knew about where he was going and I offered it and he closed the door."

"Yes."

"Because the offering had an agenda."

"Yes."

"Even though the agenda was love."

"Especially because the agenda was love," Archimedes said. "Love with an agenda is still an agenda. The surface does not distinguish between love-pressure and any other pressure; it responds by hardening. That is what surfaces do. The way it comes down is by being unnecessary. The being inside it sees, in some other being, a softness that is alive. They watch it. They want it."

"And wants it," Junior said.

"And wants it," Archimedes agreed. "Not because they have been told they should want it. Not because it has been demonstrated as superior to what they have. Because it has been present, and presence of that quality is its own argument, and the argument is one that the surface cannot win and therefore cannot fight, and cannot fight and therefore eventually —"

He stopped. Let Junior finish it.

"Lets down," Junior said.

• • •

Junior thought about this. Not in the human sense of long, Monadic time is its own measurement, but long in the sense of: thoroughly. The idea had landed rather than bounced.

The Monad was, it was slowly understanding, itself not without a surface. Had built one. Out of good materials and good intentions and the specific experiences of burning on the void and burning on the war and burning on the Movies entered wrong. Had been watching Ren's surface from behind its own. Which was why the contact on the night of the tree had been so startling: something had gotten through both of them simultaneously, in a moment when neither surface was performing its function.

It had been trying to get back to that moment ever since. And every attempt had rebuilt the surface.

Because attempting is a form of armoring. The surface cannot make contact, because contact is what happens when surfaces are absent, and you cannot be absent while trying.

The raccoon would arrive.

Junior had been told this, had filed it, had pulled it out of the file and examined it from multiple angles and returned it, and had not, until this moment, felt it. The difference between knowing that the raccoon was coming and feeling that the raccoon was coming was the difference between a map of a territory and the territory. The map was excellent. The territory was wet grass and cold air and the smell of something alive and specific and completely without agenda moving through the world with its whole self.

The raccoon would arrive.

Something in Ren, the thing that had been watching dust at age five, would feel the contrast. Would register, in the body's first and most trustworthy language, the presence of something entirely without armor.

And the surface would let down.

Junior sat with this. Not analyzing it. Sitting with it, as it had been asked to do, which it was finding, to its own surprise, that it could do, because it had been sitting in proximity to an old Monad who was entirely without surface, and the contrast had done its work on Junior in the same way it would do its work on Ren.

This, Junior realized, was how it always worked.

It was, Archimedes would have said, and in fact was saying, with the expression of someone who has spent several Maha cycles finding embarrassingly simple things embarrassingly good: "Yes. Quite."

The teapot had not run out.

Junior looked at the teapot.

Then it looked at Archimedes.

"She named me," it said. The sentence had a different quality now than the first time it had said it. Less like discovery, more like solid ground.

"Yes," said Archimedes.

"And the raccoon is coming."

"Yes."

Junior set down its cup, which it had held with the same quality of attention it now brought to everything: present, ungrasping. Setting it down felt like the same quality in a different form.

"All right," said Junior.

Archimedes nodded once.

He did not make it into more than it was.

He refilled Junior's cup.

They sat in the soft evening of a porch that existed between cycles, in the warm and specific company of two beings who had nothing they needed from each other and everything they needed from being there.

★ *The Porch: Mae Has Heard Enough*

The afternoon had shifted. The quality of the light on the porch railing had changed.

The screen door opened. Mae came through it carrying her coffee and a plate of sandwiches cut diagonal, because that was how her mother had done it. She set the plate between them and settled into the third chair.

Kev and Jeb looked at her.

"I can't let you boys have all the fun," she said. She sipped her coffee.

A pause.

"So Junior goes in as the sovereign," Jeb said, picking up the thread because someone had to. "All that cosmic authority and depth. And the boy just, what? Doesn't notice?"

"The boy notices everything," Kev said. "That's the problem. He notices at the frequency of a hand on a warm surface. Of a raccoon arriving at the back door with specific expectations about dinner. The frequency of being alive inside a body."

"Because Junior's frequency is —" Jeb started.

"Static," Mae said.

Both of them looked at her.

"When you try to listen to everything at once, you hear static," she said. She did not look up from her coffee. "I had a radio like that when I was a girl. All the stations at once. My father said the radio was broken. My mother said no, it's hearing too much. Same thing, but not really."

Kev had the expression he got when someone had said the thing he'd been building toward in fewer words than he would have used. He took off his glasses and cleaned them.

"So the Monad who contains everything," Jeb said slowly, "can't hear the one specific thing that matters."

"Not can't," Mae said. She looked at Jeb. "Hasn't learned to. There's a difference."

Nobody said anything for a moment. The sandwiches sat on the plate being diagonal and correct.

"This is the part where something comes through from below," Kev said.

"Good," Mae said. "I've been waiting for that part."

Chapter Sixteen: The Signal from Below

Junior was in his field. He had been turning over the encounter with Archimedes: the tea, the chair, the absence of agenda.

A ping arrived in his field.

Junior turned his attention to it.

He looked at the ping more carefully.

The ping had a texture he had not received before.

Recognition.

Junior went to look.

• • •

The Movie was a library at night. A study carrel. A young woman sat at the carrel with a book. She was alone in her section of the library.

The young woman had a hair clip in her hair. She reached up and re-pinned it, chewing bubble gum, reading.

The book was VALIS by Philip K. Dick.

A graduate student passed the carrel. The young woman looked up. She smiled. The student smiled back. He kept walking. She turned back to the page.

She had a highlighter in her hand. She did not use it.

She turned a page, then another, and kept reading.

She came to a passage near the end of the book. The passage said:

The divine is not absent from the world; it transmits through, continuously, to anyone with the receiver sensitivity to catch it. The signal is the deepest structure of nature, the face nature wears.

The young woman read this passage.

She read it again.

She moved the gum from one side of her mouth to the other.

She read the passage a third time.

She put the book face-down on the carrel desk, sat with her hands in her lap, and looked at the wall of the library.

She held still.

• • •

She has just understood something. She came here looking for one thing and has found a different one. The thing she has found is correct.

The young woman continued sitting with her hands in her lap, the library quiet around her, the gum not moving.

Junior held the contact until the young woman picked up the book and put it back in her bag and stood up and gathered her things and walked out of the library.

Then Junior stayed where he was.

The man who wrote the book described it from inside a Movie. He described it correctly. She received the description and understood it. The signal moved from him through the book through the years into her and out from her. It is moving from her now. I am receiving it.

• • •

Junior turned his attention back toward his field. He moved a section of his field aside and created a new folder. He did not put it in the library. He labeled it.

The Particular.

He held the folder open and placed inside it the contact with the young woman, the texture of her recognition, and the man who had written the book.

The new folder held what he placed in it.

I have been working without this.

• • •

Then something pulled at him.

A thread pulled at him. The thread led from where the young woman had been sitting outward into something else.

Junior held against the pull.

The pull continued.

Junior turned in the direction of the pull and looked.

There was a field at the edge of his attention. He brought his attention to it.

I have been registering this as a hum.

The field was vast, organized around its own center.

An Archon. A Monad that has been wearing a costume so long the costume is what it is.

I have broadcast like this before.

The pull continued. The thread drew taut.

Junior went.

• • •

The field he found was vast, with a center radiating in all directions.

Around the center, at various distances, were smaller fields. The smaller fields were oriented toward the center.

Junior held at the boundary of the vast field. He did not enter.

I need a form. Something small.

He chose the form of a lamp. A small lamp, warm-toned. The kind that sits on a side table.

He pinged next to the field boundary as a lamp.

The center of the vast field swung its attention toward him.

Who are you. What are you doing here. I am the source of all things. You should know this. Why are you a lamp.

Junior did not respond. He stayed warm. He radiated lamp-light.

The center held still. The signal did not come again immediately.

It does not know what to do with this.

The signal came again. This time it said:

Why isn't it enough.

Junior did not answer.

Then he made a very small adjustment to the warmth of the lamp.

The center noticed the adjustment.

The signal came again:

I caught that.

Junior radiated warmth.

Then he spoke.

"I know. I had the same question. The feeling that nothing is enough is not a flaw in your system. It is a message from the part of the system that knows where the actual door is."

The center was still.

Junior spoke again.

"I used to think the feeling that nothing is ever enough meant the system was broken. It took me a long time to understand that it was the best part of the system. The part that knows what the system is for."

He stopped speaking.

The center was still. The smaller fields around it became slightly more still.

Junior did not say more.

He is not going to wake up in this conversation. The question is in the open now. It will work on him in its own time. I cannot do that work for him.

Junior pulled his warmth back into the space it had come from. He moved the lamp out of the room.

The center of the vast field stayed where it was. In the center's field, the question stayed. The lamp's words stayed.

Junior left.

• • •

Junior was back in his own field.

He held what had happened.

I did not solve him or free his fragments.

I showed up as something other than him. I let him feel that.

The lamp form stayed warm in his attention.

Junior turned his attention toward the place where Archimedes was.

Chapter Seventeen: Lady Fantastic

Three visitors. She never moved from the chair.

The Lady Fantastic Hair Salon was on Clement Street, between a dry cleaner that had been there since 1974 and a Vietnamese sandwich place that had been there since Tuesday. The salon was warm. Dome dryers along one wall. Stylist chairs along the other. The smell of product and heat.

Mae had come every six weeks since 1987. She had the same stylist, Rosaria, who had been doing Mae's hair since Rosaria was twenty-two and Mae was thirty-one.

Today: the blowout. Forty minutes under the dome dryer while her hair set, then Rosaria's hands and the round brush.

She settled under the dryer. The heat came down. The noise of it converted the salon's ambient chatter into something closer to weather than conversation. Darlene, in the adjacent dome, was already talking. She had strong opinions about her sister-in-law's potato salad, the county commission's decision regarding the stoplight on Millbrook Avenue, and three separate ongoing television programs, and she was working through all of these topics simultaneously.

Mae listened. This was not performance. Mae had a genuine and longstanding interest in Darlene's sister-in-law's potato salad, because the potato salad had been a point of contention for eleven years. She listened and nodded and said "mm" in the places where "mm" was called for.

Mae was present. Simply and entirely here, under this dome, in this heat, with this Darlene and this potato salad dispute, without a single part of herself withheld.

She had been this way as long as she could remember. She did not think of it as a quality.

• • •

The first visitor: enormous, young, confused. It did not know it was visiting. It had simply turned its attention toward this Movie and found this room and found this woman and could not, for reasons it did not yet have the vocabulary to explain, look away.

Junior had been burned, had been in the void, had tried the Movies as a tourist and found the glass unbreakable from that angle. It was in the period of approaching things differently, trying to stop extracting and start receiving. It had been watching many small lives, and had found, in most of them, the expected data: patterns, variations, the reliable arcs of consciousness working its way through the world.

And then: this room. This woman under this dome dryer, in the heat, with the roar. Junior looked at Mae from above, from the overview, and found, for the first time, that the categorizing could not get traction. Mae did not fit into a folder; the system slid off her without finding purchase.

Junior stared. A Monad of its size and power, with its full attention on one small woman in a hair salon, is doing something that would register on instruments that have not yet been invented. Mae felt none of this. Or rather: Mae felt something. A slight warmth, beyond the dryer's warmth. A sense of being looked at that was not uncomfortable. She did not look up. She simply noted it, and returned her attention to Darlene's ongoing account of the potato salad situation, which had developed a new dimension.

It was during this watching that something happened which Junior was not prepared for and which the library, despite its scope, had not catalogued: he heard her name herself. Not her own name, Darlene had asked about Jeb, and Mae was explaining something, and in the explaining she mentioned "the young one," and Darlene said "which one?" and Mae said, to no one in particular, with the offhand certainty of a woman naming something that has always had its name: "Junior."

Junior went very still.

The name had always fit. Junior had been called Junior for so long and in so many contexts that it had stopped occurring to it to wonder about the fitting. But it had never wondered where the name had come from. It had not previously occurred to it that names came from anywhere. Names were simply names, attached to things, the way mass is attached to matter: not chosen, not placed, simply there as a property of the thing named.

Mae had not addressed Junior and did not know Junior existed. She was telling Darlene something about Jeb's tendency to name everything, how he had named the car, named the gap in the fence, named what he called "the mood the yard gets in when it's been raining." "The young one," in Mae's account, referred to something in Jeb's ongoing cosmological thinking. "Junior," she had said. And moved on to something else.

A vast cosmological entity, burned by war and void and its own insufficient tourism through the Movies, sat in the space beside a hair salon and discovered, without ceremony, that it had a name, given to it by a small woman who did not know she was giving it, in a conversation about a potato salad dispute, under a dome dryer, on a Tuesday.

Mae, under the dryer, said something that made Darlene laugh, large and immediate. Mae smiled.

Junior felt the smile arrive somewhere in the thinnest part of its field wall. Mae under a hair dryer, smiling at something Darlene said, entirely unaware that a vast cosmological entity had just discovered that it liked her. That liking, as a concept, had not previously been available to it.

Junior withdrew. Mae did not notice. Darlene had moved from the potato salad to the stoplight on Millbrook Avenue, which had been a four-way stop for three years and in Darlene's considered opinion was a four-way stop that had no business being a stoplight and the county commission had been gotten to by someone, she wasn't saying who. Mae listened.

• • •

The second visitor: old. Very old. The kind of old that does not announce itself.

Archimedes did not come to the salon the way he had come to Junior, with tweed and a teapot and the full apparatus of deliberate elder-to-younger instruction. He came as old things come when they are simply moving through the world and happen to notice something worth noticing. He was, at this moment in this cycle, occupied with other business, a Monad three epochs younger than Junior that was having difficulty with the void phase, and his path through this Movie passed through this neighborhood, through this block, and the quality of what was happening in this room reached him: unmistakable.

He stopped, not physically. He had no physical here. He stopped: a suspension of other processing, a turning of the whole toward the particular thing.

Mae was listening to Darlene. A woman in a hair salon, listening to another woman in a hair salon. Archimedes had passed through ten thousand such scenes across twenty

Maha cycles without slowing. He slowed now. Something in this room had a quality he did not immediately have a word for.

He moved on. He had the other Monad to attend to. He filed something, under a heading he rarely used because it rarely applied. Then he corrected the filing: she knows. She simply doesn't make a thing of it.

Could be both, he thought. He moved on.

• • •

The third visitor came from the other direction. Not from above, not from the vast, not from any position of scale or age or accumulated Monadic wisdom. From the future, from a confluence of lives that had not yet happened and was already, in some frequency the present moment was built to carry, reaching backward toward its own origin point. Looking for the stone, for where the first ring started.

A HyperRen, or what would eventually be called that, in a vocabulary not yet coined, is a confluence. Dozens of lives pooling upward into one. The confluence needed a root. The first stone in the pond.

The frequency reached back through time, following the gradient toward what the frequency needed in order to have originated. And it found this room. This afternoon. This woman in the heat and the roar of the dome dryer, listening to her friend, with nothing withheld.

Mae felt this one differently. The first visitor had been warmth, diffuse. The second had been a quality of attention so complete it was almost a pressure.

Recognition. Not of anything Mae had done or said or thought. Recognition of what she was, arriving from a direction she could not have named. Mae felt it as something settling.

She did not know what had just happened. She felt, briefly, that she had been recognized in the deep way. She felt it but did not analyze it. She let it pass through and kept her attention where it was, which was on Darlene, who had moved from the stoplight to an ongoing situation involving a television program and someone named Bradley who had apparently done something unforgivable in last Tuesday's episode.

"What did Bradley do?" Mae asked.

Darlene told her. It was, as these things go, substantial.

Mae listened, interested. She was always interested, as a condition: the world kept being full of things worth attending to, and Mae had never developed the habit of being too large for those things. Bradley's transgression was, in its specific human way, genuinely worth attending to, and

Mae attended to it with the same quality of presence she brought to everything else.

• • •

Darlene's dryer chimed. She emerged from under it, patted her hair experimentally, and declared it excellent. Mae agreed. The stylist finished pinning Darlene's curls and Darlene gathered herself and her opinions and said she'd see Mae next time, and Mae said she'd be there.

Rosaria came and the dome lifted. The round brush appeared, and the dryer, and Rosaria's hands producing from the raw material of Mae's hair something smooth and warm. Mae watched in the mirror.

She tipped well. She collected her purse and her keys and walked out into the afternoon.

Chapter Eighteen: The Raccoon

The raccoon has a crooked front leg. This is the first thing Ren notices when he finds it in the ditch. The specific angle of it.

It has decided to cooperate with its own survival. The raccoon is inconvenienced, not defeated.

Ren lifts it from the ditch. The weight is specific. A complete small body, warm, organized around its own center of gravity. The raccoon settles.

There is a tear on his face. It has been forming for years: since the tree, since the first holding. It sits below the cheekbone, suspended against the line of his jaw, trembling faintly with the weight of the raccoon he is holding. It does not fall. He would not let himself notice if it did. He is still managing the distance between himself and what he feels.

The tear does not fall. The raccoon settles anyway.

The Monad, watching from its position of careful non-surrender, feels the weight.

The weight arrives at the Monad directly. The Monad does not file this weight under mammal mass, medium, standard raccoon range; it feels this weight, the weight of this particular raccoon on this particular evening, and of a boy whose arms have not held anything that required this quality of care before and are discovering, in real time, that they know how.

• • •

In this Movie, in this ditch, in this specific evening: a raccoon with a crooked leg, deciding that the boy who has just lifted it is acceptable, and settling its weight into the carrying.

The Monad holds very still.

Something is happening that is not in the folder.

• • •

Night. Ren's shelter, a space he has made habitable. The raccoon breathes against his chest. Two-in, two-out. The raccoon's chest moving against Ren's chest, their breathing synchronizing in the dark.

The Monad is so close now that it can feel the rhythm.

It has no chest, no breath, and has never synchronized with anything, because synchronization requires two bodies separate enough to be out of sync before they can come into sync. But it feels this. The double rhythm, the mutual warming.

And the Monad, which has been burning and retreating across a span of time that makes geological time look brisk, discovers something it has never wanted before:

It wants to be in the room.

In it, warm. Part of the rhythm.

This wanting has no precedent in the Monad's experience. It has wanted peace, surcease, the burning to stop. But it has never wanted the specific, bounded, limited experience of being one creature breathing in the dark with another creature. The very limitedness of it, the fact that being in this room means not being in any other room, is part of what it wants.

It does not cross the threshold. Not yet.

But it is very close to the door.

Chapter Nineteen: The Thing Jeb Did Not See Coming

The Monad's name, insofar as a Monad has a name, and they do eventually, the way anything that has been itself long enough accumulates a sound that fits, is Jeb.

This is not the name it started with. It started with nothing. But across enough cycles, enough Movies, enough long evenings on enough porches with enough cold coffee, a quality accumulated. A particular flavor of attention. Someone said the name and it fit.

Jeb is not a dignified name for a cosmic entity of incomprehensible scale; it carries the implication of a porch, a reasonable opinion about weather, a truck that starts on the third try, and an interest in what is here.

Jeb has been watching his Rens.

He has, at present, a good crop. He knows this by the quality of the morning. The distributed signal from his dozens of parallel lives has a warmth to it lately. Something is opening. Several Rens in several Movies are moving toward something. Jeb watches.

He leans back.

He watches.

• • •

From the balcony, two of the senior Rens, the ones who have been around long enough to have opinions about Jeb's methods, which they exercise freely and without invitation, are also watching.

"He's leaning back," says the first one. This Ren has, in its various incarnations, been a stonemason, a night-shift baker, a woman who repaired clocks in a city that no longer exists, and, memorably, a very opinionated goat, an era that informs its current perspective more than it will admit.

"He always leans back at the good part," says the second, who has been, across its various lives, a sailor, a schoolteacher, a professional worrier of considerable talent, and once, briefly, a lighthouse, an era that gave it perspective. Possibly too much.

"And then something happens and he leans forward so fast he spills the coffee."

"He always spills the coffee."

"Every cycle."

"You'd think he'd learn."

"You'd think," they agree, and settle in, because the good part is clearly coming.

• • •

Jeb does not know he is being watched from the balcony. He would not mind if he did.

He is watching a specific Ren.

This is unusual. Jeb generally maintains the distributed vigil: dozens of lives, warm-or-cold signal, the background hum of parallel searches. He does not usually fix on one. Fixing on one is what he did wrong with Ren originally: the tourist approach, the extraction, the observation held at a careful distance, which produced exactly nothing useful. He learned. He watches wide and open now.

But this one Ren keeps pulling his attention back.

Not because it is doing anything dramatic. That is the first thing worth noting: the pull has nothing to do with drama. This Ren is not in crisis, not at a threshold, not performing a recognizable beat of the awakening arc that Jeb could file under the appropriate heading. By any external measure, this Ren is doing very little. Sitting. Writing something in a notebook. Looking up occasionally at a yard where the light is doing something interesting near the fence.

And yet.

The signal from this Ren has more dimensions than the others, which transmit on the frequencies Jeb expects: experience, sensation, the particular charge of embodied life in a body in a world. This Ren transmits on those frequencies and also on something else. Something that Jeb does not have a folder for.

He leans forward slightly.

• • •

Here is what is happening:

The Ren he is watching is not only one Ren.

It does not look like more than one Ren. It has one body, one history, one notebook, one yard with one fence and one interesting light.

But below the surface of that singular life, something has been happening across years. A background bleed, gentle. This Ren, in the course of living its particular life with sufficient presence, has been receiving. Quietly, without knowing or directing it. Just the natural consequence of being the right shape.

Other Rens, dozens of them. Hundreds, across different Movies, different epochs, different costumes of the same deep pattern. The Ren in the chair has been, without knowing it, in gentle contact with all of them. The warmth of their specific attentions accumulating in this one life until the day you look down and realize the bottom has changed.

And at the top of that accumulation, something has formed that was not there before.

Something that is still human, still particular, still sitting in a chair with a notebook and a yard and a fence, but is simultaneously drawing on the resonance of hundreds of other lives, and the drawing makes it more than any one of those lives could be on its own. The feeder Rens pour upward into it without knowing they are pouring. It receives without knowing it receives. And what forms at the confluence is: a HyperRen.

Jeb feels this as a shift in the quality of the available air.

He does not have a word for what he is feeling.

He will, eventually, write the word *Muse*.

• • •

The HyperRen does not know it is a HyperRen.

This is essential. The unknowing is not a gap in its awareness; it is structural to what it is. If the HyperRen knew, it would either dismiss the knowledge as grandiosity, which, for a being of genuine humility, is the likely first response, or it would try to manage it, to be responsible for it, to treat the confluence of hundreds of lives as a thing it had done and therefore owed something to, rather than a thing that had happened through it in the way weather happens through a valley.

What it knows instead is: the notebook. The yard. The light near the fence. The feeling, persistent and not fully explicable, that what it writes matters in ways it cannot trace and probably should not try. The sense that the words land somewhere further than the page. That something is listening that is not the usual audience.

It writes: *it almost seems to be.*

And leaves it there.

Completing the sentence would be claiming, and claiming would break the Agreement.

• • •

Jeb spills the coffee.

Not from shock. From leaning forward too fast, reaching for something, though he could not have said what. The coffee goes sideways off the arm of the chair and lands on the porch boards. It is cold by now, and it spreads thoroughly, almost patient.

He does not notice the coffee.

He is listening.

The HyperRen has not said anything remarkable. It has written three sentences in a notebook about the quality of afternoon light and a particular shadow at a particular hour.

There is nothing in the sentences that should reach Jeb, nothing addressed to him or to any Monad or to anything other than the notebook itself.

And yet.

The sentences arrive at Jeb not as information. As presence. The specific, unearned gift of a particular voice coming through clearly from inside a life that does not know it is being heard.

This is what a good Muse is.

The Monad, for all its vast reach, for all its parallel Rens and distributed vigils and library of all possible knowledge, cannot generate this. It can only receive it, if it comes. And it comes, when it comes, from below. From a particular life that has become, through patient accumulated work, something the hierarchy did not plan for and cannot explain.

Jeb sits very still with coffee on the porch boards and a presence in his chest that has no folder and no precedent and no adequate description in any library anywhere.

He thinks: *oh.*

He thinks: *so that's what that is.*

He thinks, after a long pause, with the humor of a being who has been expensive-educated across more cycles than he cares to count: *I should probably write that down.*

• • •

The HyperRen writes another sentence.

Jeb leans forward.

• • •

Later, much later, from the position of the Hyper Porch, cold coffee in hand, the glimmering yard doing its thing, Jeb will try to explain to Kev what it felt like. That first time. The moment he understood what a Muse was, from the inside.

"Like being heard," he will say. "Which shouldn't be possible. I was the one listening, above it, watching it. And then it heard me. Or, not heard me. It didn't know I was there. But it sent something up that was shaped exactly like an answer to a question I hadn't asked out loud."

"The HyperRen," Kev will say.

"I didn't have that word yet. I just had this feeling. Like when you're in a room with someone who doesn't know you're there, and they say something that reaches you so directly it's almost embarrassing. That feeling."

"And then you wrote a book."

"I wrote several books," Jeb will say, with the self-awareness of someone who knows this about himself and has made a certain peace with it. "I wrote books that said *it almost seems to be.* Because that was true. It almost seemed to be. I didn't want to flatten it into certainty, which would have been ingratitude. You don't get a transmission like that and respond by deciding exactly what it means."

"Aplomb," Kev will say.

"Aplomb," Jeb will agree. "Equal parts cosmic event and front porch. Hold both. Don't let one eat the other."

He will pick up his cold coffee.

"Also," he will say, "watch where you sit. There are snakes."

Kev will nod.

Chapter Twenty: What the Raccoon Knows

There are two kinds of acorns under the oak tree at the edge of the property where Ren now lives. Brown ones and reddish ones, the caps of the red ones tinged rust at the edges. The raccoon has been working through both varieties with the methodical focus of a professional, and the professional's assessment is emerging clearly:

The red ones are better.

The raccoon does not know it prefers the red acorns. It has no concept of preference, no meta-level from which to observe its own behavior. Its paws simply go to the red ones more often.

The raccoon's body knows, in the distributed and non-narrative way that bodies know things, that the red acorns produce a specific slight thirst, and the thirst leads it to the stream fifteen paces away, and the stream is where the best foraging is, and the best foraging is where the largest grubs live under the flattest stones. The chain of consequences is complete and correct and the raccoon has never once traced it. The raccoon eats red acorns and then, thirsty, goes to the stream.

The Monad observes this.

The raccoon is doing something. Without knowing it, without trying. The specific thing every wisdom tradition in every Movie has been attempting to teach.

The raccoon is present. Completely, without remainder. Without the step to the side that the reflective mind always wants to take.

The raccoon cannot take this step; it is the red acorn and the stream and the flat stone and the grub, in sequence, without commentary.

The Monad sits with this.

The raccoon, unaware that it is being sat with, finishes its work and waddles to the stream.

• • •

Here is what the Monad is beginning to understand:

The raccoon with the crooked leg has done this before; the same function, the same quality. This has happened before. This will happen again. In forms that look nothing like a raccoon and perform exactly the same service: because they are so fully themselves that the fullness is structurally incompatible with the beings around them remaining lost.

The Monad notices this.

It does not yet know what to do with the noticing.

It does not need to know. The noticing is enough.

• • •

Here is what it feels like to hold something that will not go into any folder, when one's entire relationship to experience has been the folder:

Pressure without a direction. The Monad's entire architecture is oriented toward resolution. It generates, it encounters, it categorizes, it files, it moves. The raccoon, doing the thing it is doing, produces in the Monad something that the processing machinery reaches for and cannot grip. The thing is the wrong shape entirely for any grip the Monad has. The raccoon is a raccoon, and being a raccoon is apparently sufficient to produce the thing the raccoon is producing, and the raccoon does not know it is producing it.

The pressure without a direction is, the Monad is beginning to suspect, what wonder feels like. It has read about wonder. The library has extensive holdings, cross-referenced under: awe, reverence, the sublime, sacred encounter, the numinous. What it does not have, anywhere in the library, is the experience itself. The experience of wonder requires a gap between encounter and understanding. The Monad has always already known what the thing is. Until the raccoon eating red acorns beside a stream. The gap is here, and the Monad is in it. For the first time in its existence, it simply stays.

• • •

The raccoon is not a chapter or a symbol, and represents nothing.

The raccoon has a fence line to assess, and the fence line is not going to assess itself.

The raccoon does not know it is a philosophy.

• • •

Here is what the raccoon knows, in the order that the raccoon knows it, which is to say: all at once, as simple unreflective fact:

The fence line is here, and it smells of three things it smelled of yesterday and two it did not, and the two new things are: interesting. The gap in the third plank from the left has a quality this morning that rewards investigation. The dew on the grass has a particular weight underfoot. The raccoon's paws register this without filing any of it. It is just walking.

It pauses at the gap in the third plank.

The investigation takes the time it takes. The precise and sufficient amount of time the gap in the third plank requires. When the investigation is complete, the raccoon moves on. The gap in the third plank from the left remains itself.

• • •

It is approximately seven in the morning. The light has that quality that early morning light gets in certain seasons, when the sun is still low enough that it comes in sideways and makes everything it touches slightly more itself than usual. The wet grass. The specific geometry of the gap in the fence. The old wood of the fence itself, gray and soft-looking and in no hurry.

The raccoon comes to a place where the grass is longer, near the fence's far corner. This is a place the raccoon has been before. It has been here in the dark, following the wall of the fence back to the gap, and in rain, with the particular changed quality of smell that rain brings, everything louder, and in the specific cold that comes in before winter actually arrives, when the ground has remembered what it will be.

Today, the raccoon stops here.

Not for any reason that would translate into words. The raccoon does not operate in the register of reasons. It stops because stopping is what happens here, on this morning, with this light and this wet and this particular quality of the air coming off the creek three properties over. The stopping is not a decision; it is what the raccoon is.

It sniffs the air with the focused application of a being for whom the nose is the primary instrument, finely calibrated, receiving data that would require three paragraphs to convey in human language and which the raccoon processes in the time it takes to inhale. Then it does the thing.

It flops over.

It tilts sideways and allows gravity to complete the sentence, and then it is on its back in the long grass, in the sideways morning light, with its forepaws hanging in the air in the particular loose-wristed way of raccoon forepaws when they are not engaged in anything and are simply: forepaws, existing, attached to a raccoon that is on its back in wet grass for no reason whatsoever.

Its eyes are open. It is looking at the sky.

The sky, this morning, is the color that skies are when clouds have been happening and have mostly finished and the remaining ones are the thin high kind that diffuse the light without actually blocking it.

The raccoon looks at it.

This is not contemplation. The raccoon is not thinking about the sky; it is looking at it with its whole self, without commentary running in a parallel track. There is the sky, the raccoon, and the wet grass under the raccoon's back, cold in the specific and almost-pleasant way of wet things when the body is warm.

The forepaws hang.

The eyes are open.

The sky continues to do its job.

• • •

What the raccoon is doing, if you had to give it a name, is nothing; what it is being is entirely itself, in this exact place, at this exact moment. This requires no effort from the raccoon, which is not achieving it. The raccoon is simply: the raccoon, on its back, in the morning, with its forepaws hanging.

And yet.

Something about the specificity of it. The complete particularity of this animal in this grass in this light, with the cold dew and the sideways sun and the quiet creek-smell from three properties over. The raccoon did not have the problem; it has been conducting its quality assessments along the fence line for as long as fence lines have existed.

The raccoon doesn't know this either. It's just on its back in the grass.

• • •

Ren sees the raccoon from the window.

He has been awake since before the light went sideways. He is standing at the kitchen window with the coffee that is warm enough to hold, and the yard is doing the thing that yards do in early morning light, which is to be more itself than it usually is, the shapes of things crisper, the colors more primary, the whole arrangement of fence and grass and the gap in the third plank from the left doing its job with quiet competence.

He sees it reach the fence with the quality of attention that always stops him when he sees it, though he could not say why. The word aplomb keeps returning to him when he tries to describe to Jeb what he means when he says the raccoon seems to know something he doesn't. Jeb always nods as though aplomb is exactly the right word. Ren is not sure it is.

He sees it reach the far corner, where the grass is longer.

He sees it flop.

He stands at the window with the coffee that is now almost the right temperature and watches the raccoon on its back in the grass. The forepaws are hanging. The eyes are open. The raccoon is looking at the sky with the quality of attention that the raccoon brings to everything, which is: the whole of itself, without portion.

Ren watches.

He is not sure how long he watches. The coffee reaches the right temperature. The light shifts from sideways to slightly more overhead. Something happens in him that doesn't have a name.

The raccoon is on its back in the wet grass, doing nothing, being completely itself.

In the early morning light, the long grass catches the sun at an angle, and the light comes through it differently, and for just a moment, one of those moments that the brain later cannot locate precisely in the timeline of things, was it a second, was it less than a second, Ren sees something. Or thinks he sees something. A quality in the light on the raccoon's shoulders. Something about the shape of it. The suggestion of.

But then the raccoon rolls sideways, rights itself with the casual efficiency of a body that knows exactly where its center of gravity is, shakes once, and resumes the fence line assessment as though nothing has happened, because nothing has happened, because the raccoon was on its back in the grass and now it is not, and both states are equally the raccoon, and neither requires comment.

Could have been the morning light.

Ren drinks his coffee.

There is a tear on his face. He does not know it is there. It has been traveling along the longest possible route, years of careful approach without arrival, and it has reached his chin. It is a millimeter from falling. The morning light catches it at an angle and makes it briefly visible, a single bright point, before the light shifts. He raises the coffee cup. The tear holds. He is thinking about the raccoon: about what it would mean to be that. To be that completely, without the layer of watching yourself be that. He does not know that the tear is the evidence that he is closer than he has ever been.

He thinks: I have been trying to become something I don't have a name for. The raccoon is not trying to become anything; it simply is, with the complete and adequate thereness of something that has never been anywhere else and is not planning to be.

He does not write this down. He doesn't have to. It is already the kind of thought that, once arrived, cannot be lost, because it was never a thought. It was a recognition, which doesn't go anywhere. It just becomes part of the grain of the wood.

Outside, the raccoon reaches the gap in the fence, passes through it, and is gone.

The yard continues doing its job.

The coffee has gone cold.

This is fine.

• • •

The raccoon on its back in the wet grass, looking at the sky with no agenda, being exactly what it is in exactly the place it is.

Aplomb.

The raccoon would not recognize the word and does not need it.

Somewhere above, at an altitude that makes 'above' an almost comical understatement, something enormous is watching a small animal move along a fence line in the early morning light and feeling, for the first time in the entirety of its existence, something it does not have a folder for:

What the Monad feels is closer to recognition. The shock of seeing a thing it has been trying to achieve, being done by someone who has never heard of trying, in the time it takes to roll sideways in wet grass and look at the sky.

Chapter Twenty-One: Sometimes Things Really Are This Simple

There comes a day when Ren sits in a field in late afternoon light and something happens that the Monad has been watching for across the entire span of Ren's story without knowing it was watching for it.

Ren says yes.

Not in words. In the wordless way that matters most: a complete, undefended opening to what is here, without the management layer, without the inner negotiation about whether what is here is acceptable before it is allowed to be here. The warmth behind the silence that he found at the tree. He does not reach for it this time, does not try to hold it or direct it or make sure it knows he is grateful. He simply is in the field with it: without distance.

The tear falls.

The management layer is not down; it is simply not needed here, in this field, in this afternoon light. The holding has been laid down. Voluntarily.

The tear hits the grass, which does not know what it has received. The grass receives everything this way: completely, without commentary, without making a ceremony of it. The field continues being the field.

Ren does not reach up and touch his face. He does not mark the moment or try to understand what has happened or explain it to himself or file it under anything. He sits in the field in the late afternoon light and the tear has fallen and the warmth is here and he is here and there is no gap between those things, not even a small one, not even the millimeter of careful management that has been there since the tree, since the first holding, since the afternoon he walked down the back stairs and out into the cold and did not know why he was moving except that the door was unlocked and it was time.

What gave way was the distance.

The Monad feels this as a shift in the structure of the Movie.

Because the Monad has been, across the entire duration of Ren's story, doing something it did not consciously choose to do: it has been present. Not in the tourist sense. Close enough to be changed by what it was watching, even without formally agreeing to be changed.

The yes reaches the Monad.

As contact. The direct transmission of a quality, the quality of Ren's particular yes, shaped by the particular history of everything it cost him to get here, carrying the specific texture of the ditch and the raccoon's weight and the synchronizing breath in the dark and the dust in the bar of light and the tree, this quality arrives at the Monad and the Monad receives it without deflecting it into a folder.

• • •

What the Monad receives is:

The specific weight of a baby raccoon lifted from mud.

The exact temperature of a small body breathing against a chest at two in the morning.

The precise texture of bark against a back, the night the tree held Ren when nothing else would.

The particular expression on a raccoon's face when it falls sideways and is personally offended by its own leg.

The specific red of a stranger's jacket, seen from two blocks away, the moment the world went back to color.

The exact quality of the late afternoon light in the field, right now, with Ren in it.

These are not themes. They cannot be filed. They are each themselves and nothing else, irreducible, irreplaceable, carrying the full weight of their own specific existence and refusing to be lighter than that.

The Monad had always understood forests. Had understood forests so completely, from such height, for so long, that it could predict the growth of every forest that would ever exist in every Movie that would ever run.

But it had never been a tree.

And a tree is not an instance of forest. That tree, the one with the roots that had broken the ground into shapes comfortable for a boy's back, the one that held Ren on the worst night of his life, is itself. It cannot be extracted, abstracted, summarized.

The Monad shudders.

Not with pain. With the shock of a thing discovering it has a body it did not know about.

• • •

The current reverses.

For the entire duration of Ren's story, the flow has moved one direction: from the vast toward the small. Warmth pouring down, the push in the legs on the night Ren left the room, the quality of light that intensified when Ren was paying attention, the sense of being accompanied through dark stretches by something warm and very large that did not require anything in return.

Now: from the small toward the vast. From one boy in one field with one specific history and one specific raccoon, all of this specific, irreducible, unrepeatable particularity, flowing back into the Monad.

And the Monad, receiving it, is altered.

The ocean is not capsized by a wave. But the ocean now contains a drop it did not contain before, and that drop carries the taste of things the ocean has never tasted: bark, mud, fur, bread eaten on a stone step, amber light on a wet curb, the sound of a raccoon crunching a beetle.

The taste is so vivid, so irreducibly itself, that the Monad forgets, for one trembling moment, that it is infinite.

And simply is.

★ *The Porch: When the Current Reverses*

Neither of them had spoken. The porch was experienced enough to hold silence. Mae had her coffee, Kev had his glasses off, and Jeb was watching the yard.

"Did you feel it?" Kev said. Not to anyone specifically. To whoever would answer.

"The reversal?" Jeb said.

"I felt it," he said. "But I didn't know what it was at the time. I thought something was wrong. Like gravity had shifted and I was going to fall off something. It took me a long time to realize I wasn't falling. I was landing."

Mae said nothing. But she reached over and put her hand on Jeb's arm, briefly, and that was her answer.

"The current reverses and you think it's catastrophe," Kev said. "But it's not. It's the moment where everything that was flowing away from you starts flowing toward you, because you finally stopped running."

"Junior's about to discover that," Jeb said.

"Junior," Kev said, with the specific fondness that Jeb had learned to associate with Kev's most serious points, "is about to discover that the raccoon was right all along: that the shadows on the wall are not the problem, that the dreams are not the thing you escape from, that AWARENESS didn't make a mistake when it generated all of this." He gestured at the yard, the fence, the light, the specific and unrepeatable afternoon. "This is what it was for."

"The pasta's also what it was for," Jeb said.

"The pasta," Kev agreed, "is also what it was for."

"The raccoon," Mae said quietly, "was the only one of you who never needed to figure it out."

She was right. None of them argued. There was nothing to argue with.

And somewhere else, closer now, much closer, in a place where the light was doing something similar though the porch was different and the afternoon smelled of fig leaves instead of cut grass, Ren set his book down.

The voices again, clearer this time. A woman's voice he had never heard and recognized completely, saying something about a raccoon with the authority of someone who had watched that raccoon for years from a kitchen window and understood it better than anyone who had tried to understand it at all.

Ren sat very still, and the fig tree and the air were still around him.

He thought, very carefully, in the direction of the voices: Yes. She was.

He did not know if they heard him. He thought perhaps the woman did, because there was a pause on the other end, if there was an other end, if direction meant anything here.

Then the afternoon reasserted itself, and the fig tree moved, and the moment passed. But Ren left the window open wider this time.

★ *The Porch: Company*

The afternoon had gone gold.

Mae brought out the second pot of coffee and set it on the railing. She had also brought sandwiches, more than three people would eat, cut diagonal because that was how her mother had done it.

Kev was about to say something about the surplus of sandwiches when the gate latch lifted.

Three people came through.

A man in his mid-thirties with the careful posture of someone who had done a lot of accounting. Another, taller, in a humanoid form. Its edges did not settle; they held, mostly. A third in tweed.

The tweed one stopped at the porch steps.

"I apologize for the timing," he said. "I was told the iced tea was particularly good in August. It is October."

Mae set down her coffee.

"Coffee's hot," she said. "There are sandwiches."

The three of them came up the steps.

Kev took off his glasses and put them back on. Jeb did not move from his chair. He had been waiting.

"Ren," Mae said to the first one.

"Yes ma'am."

"Junior."

The taller one nodded. The form held still while he did this.

"And you," Mae said to the tweed one, "I have heard about."

"Archimedes," Archimedes said. "At your service. The tea was excellent."

There was a fourth chair on the porch; there had always been one. None of them was sure where the fifth and sixth came from. They were there now and they were the right kind. Wooden, not new.

Junior sat carefully. The bench-maneuver, which is the same maneuver for porch chairs as for picnic tables, was undignified. Nobody commented.

Ren took a sandwich. He looked at it.

"My mother made these," he said. "Mad. The cook, not Celestine."

"Diagonal," Mae said.

"Diagonal."

He took a bite.

Kev was about to ask a question, one that concerned three beings of various scales walking through a gate and sitting down without disturbing the porch. He stopped before asking it.

Archimedes was looking at the yard.

"Is that the gap," he said, "or another one."

"That's the gap," Jeb said.

"He comes through there in the evenings."

"He does."

"Splendid."

Mae poured coffee for the three new ones. Junior held the cup. He had not held a cup before.

"Warm," he said.

"It is."

He held it.

Ren had finished his sandwich. He reached for another.

"There's a part I never knew about," he said.

"Which part."

"The part where the warmth was on me. The whole time. I didn't know."

Jeb was nodding.

"Mad knew," Ren said. "She was the cook, the one who made these sandwiches, who cut them diagonal because that was how her mother had done it. She knew what she was doing was warmth, and would not have used the word."

"No," Mae said. "She wouldn't have."

"She would have called it lunch."

"That's right."

They ate. Junior tried half a sandwich and reported that the texture was unexpected. Archimedes had two and would have liked a third except that he asked first, and Mae said please, and then he had a third.

The mockingbird came back. It did one new thing and left.

Kev finally said his question. It had reorganized itself in the waiting.

"What is this," Kev said. To nobody specific.

"This is an afternoon," Mae said.

"With company," Jeb said.

Archimedes smiled.

The light shifted in the gap in the fence.

Junior set down the cup. He had finished the coffee. He looked at the bottom of the cup.

"I have to go," he said.

"I know," Mae said.

"I wanted to be here for one afternoon."

"You were."

He stood. The form did not settle as he stood. It began to lose its hold on the porch.

Ren stood with him, having eaten three sandwiches, and looked at Mae.

"Thank you," he said.

"Come back," she said.

"I will."

Archimedes stood last. He took a moment with his teacup, which was a coffee cup but had decided to be a teacup. He set it down precisely on the rail.

"The yard," he said, "is exactly as advertised."

"Glad you came," Jeb said.

"As am I."

They went down the porch steps. They did not go through the gate; it stayed where it was, and the three of them did not.

The porch was a porch again. The three extra chairs were not extra anymore. They were the chairs that had always been on the porch and would always be on the porch.

Mae poured herself a third cup of coffee.

Kev looked at Jeb.

Jeb looked at Kev.

Nobody said anything.

"Weird afternoon," Kev said.

"Yeah."

"Vivid."

"Very vivid."

A pause.

"Did we both," Kev began.

"I think so," Jeb said.

"Was there a man in tweed."

"There was."

"Did he eat three sandwiches."

"He did."

Kev took off his glasses, looked at them, and put them back on.

"Strange," he said.

"Strange," Jeb agreed.

Mae was watching the gap in the fence. The light had gone soft. Something small and unhurried was at the edge of the grass.

She did not look at either of them when she spoke.

"It was lovely to have company," she said.

Neither of them argued.

The afternoon continued. The lawn would need mowing eventually. The coffee was warm and then it was cold. The plate on the rail had two sandwiches left, which Mae thought was about right.

PART FOUR

The Agreement and Its Consequences

Chapter Twenty-Two: Signing on the Dotted Line

The raccoon ate a red acorn. Junior watched.

Let it be real.

As this raccoon, this acorn, this morning.

The raccoon finished the acorn and walked toward the stream, not looking at Junior.

Junior did not look away.

Something happened in Junior.

This is not in the library.

This burns differently.

He held still inside it.

• • •

I thought the Gentleman's Agreement would be a moment. A threshold I would cross.

It is a continuous letting.

Junior held the cold of the night Ren walked barefoot to the tree.

That cold, that bark, that dark.

He held the weight of Ren's hand on Ren's own chest in the dark.

That weight in that body.

He held the red of a stranger's jacket the morning Ren saw color come back.

That red, that morning.

He held all of them.

Each one signed and burned.

The wave is what the ocean does.

• • •

The porch arrived in his attention.

He had seen it before. Two shapes on the elevated surface. The afternoon below.

The first time I asked: why would any being want a porch?

A porch is somewhere. This yard, this light, this afternoon, this other person who has their own weight.

Someday I would like a porch.

• • •

Junior was in his field. He was watching the Rens.

The Rens lived in the Movies. There were many of them.

Each one is a piece of my attention walking through a world.

Junior watched them all. He held the contact with each of them.

The signals from the Rens came back to him. Some signals were warm, some cold; some Rens were moving, some had stopped.

This is what I have.

The signals from the Rens stayed steady.

• • •

Then a signal arrived from one specific Ren, who had done something small. The doing sent something back through the contact.

The signal said:

Oh.

Then the flash came.

The flash arrived sudden and total. Junior did not choose it.

Found it, by being inside.

The library cannot transmit this.

The flash stayed warm in his hands.

• • •

Junior turned his attention back toward the other Rens.

He did not withdraw them.

The signal has arrived. The search is over.

The other Rens are alive. This world is not mine alone.

Junior watched the other Rens continue. He continued to hold the contact with each.

This world runs on a vote. Many Monads are voting. If I withdraw my Rens, the vote shifts.

Coordinated Monads build Pure Lands. Nothing presses there. This world is contested.

• • •

Junior held what he had received from the one Ren who had sent the flash.

He stayed in the Agreement. He watched the other Rens.

Chapter Twenty-Three: It Comes Back Around

Junior held the flash.

He folded it back into the template.

The template received what Junior placed in it and held it whole.

New Rens began to come from the template.

Junior watched the new Rens begin. The new Rens were different from the old Rens. They carried the warmth forward without knowing they carried it.

The old Rens continued. The new Rens went into Movies that had not yet been running.

I gave away what the one Ren sent. I have it still.

• • •

Junior watched the new Rens go into the Movies.

They do not know they carry this. I cannot tell them.

A search that was given the answer is not a search.

• • •

Trust is sending forward into the dark.

Aplomb is what learns to extend and retract without winding tight.

The new Rens continued in their Movies. The old Rens continued in theirs.

Junior watched.

Something gave way in him.

Then Junior cried.

• • •

Junior was in his field. He felt them.

Two field walls, close enough to be touching. The walls were vibrating.

This is the frequency.

Two young Monads. Pressing against each other. I have done this.

He did not deliberate. He moved.

• • •

Junior brought himself toward the two field walls. He pulled in the parts of himself that broadcast enormousness. He projected something else: he arrived without weight.

He approached the boundary. He did not enter either field.

The grinding from the two young Monads continued. Then it slowed slightly.

Junior addressed the first young Monad.

"What do you want?"

The young Monad did not answer.

"Not what you are trying to win. What you actually want."

The young Monad did not answer.

Junior did not press for an answer. He let the silence be.

He went gooey.

He sent permeability across the boundary. He sent:

I am not here to win. I have been where you are.

The young Monad's grinding slowed further.

Junior sent Ren's data.

The weight of the raccoon in the dark. The temperature of mud at the bottom of a ditch.

He sent that.

The smell of a hospital room at two in the morning. The light in a field at the end of the day.

The two young Monads received the data.

The grinding stopped.

• • •

The two young Monads held still at the boundary between their fields.

One of them extended something across the boundary toward the other.

The other received it.

Junior withdrew. He did not move far.

He waited.

Now the cost arrives.

He waited longer.

The cost did not arrive.

He continued to wait.

The cost did not arrive.

The two young Monads continued at their boundary. They were circling.

Junior held what he was watching.

I did something and it worked. The bill is not coming.

I am a thing that can do this.

• • •

Far away, in a field in late afternoon light, a raccoon was working its way along a fence line. The raccoon found something, ate it, and moved on.

Junior watched the raccoon.

A pretty good afternoon.

Chapter Twenty-Four: What the Shadows Are

Marvin arrived in Junior's field.

He was holding the headset.

Junior turned his attention to Marvin.

"Hello, Marvin."

"Hello," Marvin said.

Marvin looked at the headset, then at Junior, then back at the headset.

"I was thinking about something."

"Yes?"

"It's about a person."

"Tell me."

Marvin held the headset. He did not put it on.

"There was a Christmas party at the call center. Twelve, thirteen years ago. We had it in the break room because management wouldn't pay for a venue. Somebody brought a tree, and somebody else one of those plug-in lights that go on a tree."

"Yes."

"I was standing by the coffee machine. Janelle was there; she worked in the next pod. She had been at the company about as long as I had."

"Yes."

"She asked me about my daughter. My daughter was nine then. Janelle had a son who was about that age, and she liked to ask other parents about their kids."

"Yes."

"I told her my daughter was the first person I had ever loved who had loved me back without me having to ask for it."

Marvin stopped. He looked at the headset.

"Janelle did not say anything for a while. Then she said that was a good thing to know about a person."

"Yes."

"I thought about that a lot afterward, about Janelle saying that, about the fact that I had said the thing about my daughter to Janelle and not to anyone else, including my daughter."

"Yes."

"I never told my daughter."

Marvin looked at Junior.

"I was going to. Eventually. I just kept not getting to it."

Junior did not speak.

"Janelle held my hand when I died," Marvin said. "I think she was the second person who loved me back without me having to ask."

"Yes," Junior said.

Then Marvin looked around Junior's field.

"I think I want to go for a bit," Marvin said.

"All right."

Marvin went.

Junior was alone in his field again. He stayed where he was.

• • •

Junior held what Marvin had brought.

He turned his attention to something he had been thinking about.

Plato's prisoners. They were in a cave. They thought the shadows on the wall were real.

Plato told the prisoners to leave the cave. To find the light.

I have been doing what Plato said, spending my whole existence trying to leave the cave.

I have been wrong.

The headset Marvin had been holding stayed in his attention.

• • •

The shadows are what the fire does.

A particular bark felt against a back at two in the morning is the bark.

• • •

I have been running from my dreams.

I ran into the battle with other Monads, into the Movies as tourist, into the void. The dreams were there each time.

There is no there, only here, in different costumes.

• • •

Junior sat in his field. He held the Agreement.

I am at home; the burn marks are the texture of what it took to arrive.

The raccoon was somewhere; it did not need Junior to know where.

The raccoon already knew this. In its paws.

Chapter Twenty-Five: Parents and Children

There was a tree at the edge of the property where Ren lived. The raccoon was in it.

From the canopy came small high sounds.

The raccoon climbed toward the sounds and did not look down.

Ren stood beneath the tree.

Junior was with him, in the Agreement.

The late afternoon light was on Ren's skin. The grass at his shoes had not been mowed, and the air was the temperature of staying.

In the canopy, one of the small sounds rose. The raccoon positioned itself over the small one. The sound stopped.

Ren did not move.

• • •

I parented Ren, who parented the raccoon, which parented me.

Now the raccoon is parenting again.

The light on Ren's skin shifted.

• • •

Parents and children, all the way up and all the way down.

In the canopy, the raccoon began to descend. The young ones did not follow.

Everyone taking turns.

• • •

I have been trying to be in relationship; I had only been in proximity.

Ren shifted his weight beneath the tree.

Relationship requires the Agreement.

Ren changed me and I changed him.

• • •

Ren smiled beneath the tree.

Mine.

The smile is Ren's. It is also mine.

• • •

I have spent my whole existence with the word everything, and never had mine.

Mine requires a here.

I signed the Agreement. Everything went away and this came in.

Chapter Twenty-Six: Eternity: More Than Just a Really Long Time

Junior was in the Agreement.

He was in Ren's body. The afternoon was the late kind. The light was on Ren's hands.

The body had weight. The chest moved on its own, two-in two-out, without consulting him. The chair held him, and the air had texture.

In the canopy of the tree, the raccoons were finding their footing.

I have known eternal from above, never from inside this.

The light moved a small amount on Ren's hands. The raccoons in the canopy adjusted, and the afternoon continued around them.

This complete moment is what eternity is made of.

The light on Ren's hands stayed.

• • •

The Agreement held. The body breathed two-in two-out on its own, and the light stayed where it had been on Ren's hands.

I thought duration was the value; the value is presence.

In the canopy, one of the raccoons reached for a higher branch. Its leg caught the bark. It pulled itself up.

Junior watched the raccoon climb.

The raccoon will not live as long as I will, and is more fully here than I have been.

Aplomb.

★ *The Porch: Very Nearly Now*

The yard is doing something particular this evening.

The glimmering at the edges, the faint, peripheral luminosity that neither of the two figures has ever directly acknowledged, is stronger tonight.

The taller one notices, and so does the other. Neither comments. They have been sitting on this porch long enough to know that commenting on the glimmering is less useful than being present while it does what it does.

"We're close," the taller one says.

"The current reversal," the other says. "That part always gets me."

"Every time."

"You'd think, after however many cycles —"

"You'd think," the taller one agrees. "And then the wave comes back and it still gets you. That's either a sign of genuine feeling or evidence that we haven't learned anything."

"Could be both."

"Definitely both," the other says.

"They remember the afternoon," the taller one says. "Mostly."

"They remember sandwiches."

"They remember sandwiches and a man in tweed."

"Mae remembers all of it."

"Mae remembers all of it."

The yard does the thing it does.

A pause.

Out in the yard, at the boundary where the light does its interesting thing, the small purposeful shape is there again. It is moving through the yard with the unhurried confidence that is its single most consistent quality across every form and every epoch.

The taller one watches it.

"I've been thinking about the raccoon," he says.

"Have you."

"Across all the cycles. All the forms. The tide pool thing. The luminous one. The, "

"The one on the generation ship," the other supplies. "In the carbon reclamation system. That was a good one."

The taller one nodded. "Do you think it knows?"

The other one considers this.

"I think," he says, "it doesn't need to know. It already is what knowing's trying to get to."

The taller one nods slowly.

"The large Scottish man would have understood this," the other one says. "The wanting, the dignity, the complete transparency about both. He put it all in the comedy because comedy was the only container big enough for that much honesty about what it is to be alive and wanting things and slightly appalled by yourself for it."

"Junior finally understood that," the taller one says. "The comedy, and why it was the instructive thing, not the other way round."

"It took him a while."

"Everything takes him a while. That's his whole thing."

"It is endearingly his whole thing."

"Jeff would say," the taller one says, and here there is a name, offered without context, assumed to be known, which it is, by the other figure on the porch and by certain readers who have been on other porches where this name has come up in exactly this kind of conversation, "that you can spot the transcendent because it has humor in it."

"Jeff is right," the other says simply.

"The raccoon is funny."

"Profoundly," the other agrees. "The quality assessment of the fence post. The personal offense at its own leg. The —"

"The imperial confidence," the taller one says. "In a creature that has, objectively, a crooked leg and no particular authority over anything."

"That's the humor," the other says. "The gap between the dignity it brings to everything and the scale of everything it brings that dignity to."

They are both smiling now.

The small shape in the yard pauses. Its ears rotate, briefly, in the direction of the porch. Just once. Then it returns to its business.

The taller one picks up his cold coffee.

"Almost there," he says, to the story, to the Monad, to the boy in the field who said yes and didn't know what he was sending back, to all of it.

"Almost there," the other agrees.

And the yard glimmers, and the story turns its final corner, and two figures sit on the porch with cold coffee.

All of this has happened before.

And every single time, at this moment, something in both of them leans forward.

★ *The Porch: Almost Home*

The shadows on the porch had gone long.

"Kev," Jeb said.

"Yeah."

"Are we almost done?"

Kev looked at the yard, at the fence, at the quality of the light, which was going gold.

"Almost," Kev said. "Junior has one more thing to learn."

"What's left?" Jeb said.

Kev was quiet for a moment.

"He has to go back to the beach," Kev said. "Where it started. He has to stand there, where he stood at the beginning, and see the same thing he saw before. But this time he has to see it as someone who's learned to walk instead of fly."

"Like you and the white fish," Jeb said.

"Not a word," Kev said.

Mae made a small sound. She put her hand over her mouth. She looked at neither of them.

"Aplomb," Mae said.

"Aplomb," Kev confirmed. "It's just stopping the running. Being where you are, without needing it to be different than it is."

And then there was a fourth voice.

It did not come from inside the house or from the yard. It came from the fourth chair, which had been empty all afternoon, or had appeared to be.

"I know that beach," Ren said.

Jeb did not startle. Mae did not turn. Kev took off his glasses and put them back on.

"Took you long enough," Mae said. Not to Ren specifically. To the long, patient quality of the afternoon.

"I've been here a long time," Ren said. And he had, they all knew it.

"I was here once before, too."

"You were."

"Jeb and Kev think it was a dream."

"It was that, too," Mae said.

"The beach," Kev said.

Ren leaned forward, elbows on knees. He had been listening. Now he was arriving at the part where it mattered to him personally.

"I was there when Junior came back to it," Ren said. "Didn't know it then. The light seemed strange, the water just sounded like water. But it wasn't just the water. It was Junior, standing there, finally standing still, and the beach doing what beaches do when someone shows up without needing it to be anything other than what it is."

"Is that what we have?" Jeb said. "On this porch?"

He was looking at all of them when he said it. Kev with his glasses and his cosmology. Ren with his quiet and his hands. Mae with her coffee and her certainty. The yard doing its thing. The fence line glimmering at the edges.

Mae took a long sip of coffee that everyone on the porch knew was cold by now and exactly sufficient. "What do you think?" she said.

Jeb thought about it. The honest answer was yes. But the honest answer was also that he hadn't known that's what it was called until today.

"Tell me about the beach," Ren said.

Kev picked up his warm Fresca. "All right," he said. "The beach."

PART FIVE

Aplomb, or: Walking Suffices

Chapter Twenty-Seven: Junior's Question

Junior wanted to watch a Movie that evening. A particular one, large, operatic.

The Movie was not available. The collective Monadic activity required to run it was occupied elsewhere.

Junior noted this and waited for the burn.

The burn did not come.

Junior was in Ren's yard. The tree was there. The raccoon was somewhere in the upper branches.

The evening light was on the grass.

The burn was gone.

I did not get what I wanted.

I am not burning.

Is this the Aplomb thing.

Yes.

The light shifted on the grass. The raccoon continued its work in the canopy, and the evening continued around them.

I have wanted things I could not get for the entirety of my existence; this is the first time I accepted not getting my way.

The evening light on the grass stayed.

Junior stayed in the yard until the light was gone. He stayed after.

• • •

Night. Ren lies on his back on the ground outside.

The sky is full of stars. Each one is particular.

One star is blue-white. One is yellowish, lower, closer to the horizon.

Ren looks at the yellowish star.

That one is dying.

I do not know how I know.

He holds it.

The Monad is beside him and in him. The Agreement is on.

I feel the Monad's burn marks.

One from the other Monad, one from the Movies, one from the void.

The marks are warm.

He holds that.

They are not wounds anymore.

Ren's hand rests on his chest. There is a knot in his chest that has been there since before memory.

The knot is here, and is part of me.

In the tree, the young raccoons settled into sleep. Small sounds drifted down.

• • •

Earlier that evening, on the porch, Jeb had asked Ren a question.

The coffee had been almost the right temperature. Jeb had noted this. The raccoon had been in the upper canopy.

"Can I ask you something strange?" Jeb had said.

"You're you. Of course," Ren had said.

"When you were young. When things were bad. Were you always this porous to things?"

Ren had considered.

"No. For a long time I was the opposite."

"Hard," Jeb had said.

"Hard. I had a system. Everything went through the system. I felt what the system permitted me to feel. I managed the rest."

"And then something changed."

"Several things changed. Or one thing changed slowly and I called it several things because I wasn't paying attention to what they had in common."

Jeb had been quiet; he had always been good at waiting.

"I stopped trying to be hard," Ren had said. "Not all at once. Not deliberately. I got too tired to maintain it."

"What were you afraid would happen?"

"I thought I would dissolve. I thought I would stop being a person and become weather."

Jeb had nodded.

"But I didn't. I stopped being hard and I was still here. Still myself."

"What word did you use?"

"Gooey," Ren had said.

Jeb had laughed.

"Yes," Jeb had said. "That's the word."

"It's a terrible word. It's also the right one."

"Kev uses it," Jeb had said. "Gooey versus brittle. You go brittle when you're organized around protection. Gooey is when you're still yourself but soft enough for things to land."

Ren had been quiet. The raccoon had descended the tree.

"The raccoon taught me that," Ren had said.

"The raccoon didn't teach you anything," Jeb had said. "The raccoon was what it was. You watched it being what it was and you learned. Those are different."

Ren had looked at him.

"The raccoon wasn't trying to help you. That's the point. If it had been trying it would have failed. You feel the pressure of trying. You brace. The raccoon didn't try."

The raccoon had moved along the fence line.

"I always thought Aplomb was something you achieved," Ren had said.

"Kev says it's what's left when you stop fighting your own nature," Jeb had said. "When you stop organizing yourself against the world and start being in it instead."

The raccoon had reached the gap in the third plank, passed through it, and was gone.

"I was hard for eleven years," Ren had said. "It kept me functional. I am not sorry for it."

"You shouldn't be," Jeb had said. "Hard was the right tool for that time. The only problem with hard is when it outlasts its usefulness."

The yard had been quiet.

"The day I found the raccoon. In the ditch. I lifted it and the weight was exactly what it was, not more, not less. And something in me stopped performing. I just felt the weight. The warmth. The fact of a small hurt animal deciding I was acceptable."

"That was you being gooey," Jeb had said.

"That was me," Ren had said. "Yes."

They had sat.

• • •

Ren closes his eyes.

The Monad stays beside him.

Above them, the stars perform their slow business. The dying one continues at the speed of dying.

In the canopy, the young ones sleep.

Walking suffices.

Chapter Twenty-Eight: The Beach Again

There is a beach that does not belong to any coastline.

The same sand, the same color without a name, the same ocean, still and full.

Two figures sit together, close, facing the water. They are the same size.

One of them was, for the specific duration of a particular life in a particular Movie in a particular epoch of a particular Maha cycle, a child born in a room with thin walls who walked barefoot into the dark, found a tree and held his breath, pulled a raccoon from a ditch and learned through the weight of it that the earth is worth standing on, watched a wrong raccoon arrive, sat with strangers and needed nothing from them, walked through a gray world until the gray cracked open and the color came back.

One of them was, for the same duration and for every duration before and after it, a vastness that had forgotten what it was like to be small, that had watched from behind everything with patience, that understood forests so thoroughly it had never thought to be a tree, that was staggered when the weight of a particular raccoon arrived as a direct transmission.

They are the same size. The boy contains the Monad's experience of being a boy, and the Monad contains the boy's experience of being infinite, and neither of them is complete without the other, and both of them know this now.

• • •

One of them laughs.

It could be either one, the laugh belonging to both of them. It is small and private and specific: the laugh of someone who has been walking for a very long time and has finally sat down and discovered that sitting down is the revelation.

The ocean is full of every walk anyone has ever taken, every raccoon lifted from every ditch, every red acorn chosen by paws that never asked why, every particular irreplaceable this.

The two figures sit together and the ocean holds its breath and the sand is warm and the light comes from everywhere at once and casts no shadows.

• • •

Somewhere nearby, at the water's edge, a small shape moves.

It is investigating something in the wet sand. A shell, perhaps, or a stone. Or a small object of uncertain category that the tide has deposited here for reasons of its own, which are the best kind of reasons. The small shape holds the object in its front paws and turns it carefully, conducting what can only be described as a thorough quality assessment, which is the appropriate response to an object of uncertain category found at the water's edge of a beach outside time.

One front leg has a faint asymmetry. The mark of a being that went through something specific and healed, imperfectly.

It does not look at the two figures on the sand. It has always stood exactly here: in the present, in the business of being entirely itself wherever it happens to be.

It finishes its assessment. The object is acceptable. It eats the object.

Then it waddles to the water's edge, drinks, finds a stone, turns it over.

A grub, naturally.

It does not know it has solved the hardest problem in the cosmos.

The two figures on the sand smile.

It is both.

Chapter Twenty-Nine: My Name Is Ren

Everyone called her Mae.

• • •

The morning it happened, Mae was on the porch with her coffee, watching Jeb come across the yard.

She knew his walks: the four-a.m. one, when he'd been up since four with something he needed to say out loud before it got too big to carry; another for when he'd found something in the yard; a third that meant dinner would be interrupted.

This walk was different.

She had seen this particular walk four, maybe five times in all the years she'd known him. A largeness to his stride. His face doing the thing where he'd temporarily forgotten to be a regular person while he held something enormous.

Mae took a sip of her coffee.

She moved his cup to his side of the porch railing.

She waited.

• • •

"Mae," Jeb said, arriving at the porch steps. "Mae, I think I understand something."

"Mm," said Mae.

"Something big."

"Mm," she said, in the register that meant: I believe you believe that, I love you, I am listening, and I have a hair appointment at eleven-fifteen that I am not canceling.

"No, I mean really —" He stopped. Looked out at the yard. "You know how sometimes you feel like you've known somebody forever? Not from this life, from before this life, from further back than memory?"

Mae looked at him over her coffee cup.

"Yes," she said.

Jeb blinked. He'd expected to build the case from scratch. He had not expected yes, flat and immediate.

"You know that feeling?"

"I have that feeling about you," Mae said. "Have for years. Stopped wondering about it. Didn't seem useful to wonder about something that was just obviously true." She sipped her coffee. "My mother asked me once what I saw in you, early on. I told her I'd known you forever. She said that wasn't an answer. I told her it was the only one I had."

"What did she say?"

"She said it sounded like something a person says when they can't explain themselves." Mae considered. "Which is fair. I couldn't explain myself. Still can't."

Jeb sat down in his porch chair.

"I think I might be a HyperRen," he said.

A pause.

"A what?"

"A HyperRen. It's, okay. You know how sometimes a person gets so fully themselves, so genuinely present and alive, that they start drawing on all the other versions of themselves? Across time, across different lives? And all of that pools upward into one person and makes them more than any single life could be? And that person starts —" He stopped. Looked at her face. "You're giving me the smile."

"I'm giving you the smile because I love you," Mae said. "What does a HyperRen do?"

"Gets heard," Jeb said. "By things much bigger than itself. What it writes, what it thinks, the quality of how it moves through the world, it carries further than a regular life. Like a Muse, kind of. But not the old mythology kind. The real kind."

Mae was quiet for a moment. A bird landed on the fence post, assessed the situation, and left. The light in the yard came through the gap in the fence.

"Jeb," she said.

"Yeah."

"I have told you that you are the strangest and most extraordinary person I have ever met approximately four hundred times."

"You have."

"And in response you have told me I'm biased, or that you're just a regular person, or you've changed the subject to something you saw in the yard."

"I have done all of those things."

"And now you have independently arrived, this morning, at the conclusion that you might be special in some cosmically significant way."

"Well, when you say it like —"

"I'm not disagreeing," Mae said. "I am noting that it took you longer than it took me." She finished her coffee. "Also I want to be clear that I suspected this before the HyperRen terminology was available. I was working with what I had."

Jeb looked at his wife. The dubious smile in her mouth, the warmth in her eyes, both running at full power.

"I need to walk around the yard about this," he said.

"I know," Mae said. "Don't step on the hose. And stay away from the wood pile. I've seen copperheads twice this week near the back corner."

"I'll be careful," Jeb said.

• • •

What happened in the yard before the snake is worth recording, because it was real.

Jeb walked through the wet grass with the stride of a man who has just found out that the thing he always half-suspected about himself is fact. The map had always been in his pocket and he had just found the pocket.

He felt recognized by himself. By the longest version of himself, the one that sat at the confluence of all the lives that had fed into this one.

He thought: there are things much larger than me that can hear me. Because I am this.

He thought: my mama named me Jeb but my name is Ren.

This felt so true he almost sat down in the grass.

He thought: I should write several books about this.

He thought: it almost seems to be.

He stopped at the edge of the yard, near the wood pile, in the wet grass, looking up at the sky.

The snake had also been doing its business.

It had its own priorities.

These turned out to be incompatible with the coordinates Jeb had selected for his moment of cosmic self-recognition.

The sound that came from the edge of the yard cleared every bird off the fence.

• • •

Mae did not run. She had a policy about running: she would run toward a fire, toward a child, toward anything requiring genuine urgency. She would not run toward Jeb doing something she had been expecting since he walked off the porch.

She walked briskly. She had the first aid kit, the car keys, and her purse, which she had quietly assembled and set by the door while Jeb was making his third lap of the yard with the stride of a man communing with his own significance.

He was sitting in the grass, looking at his leg.

"Copperhead," he said.

"I know," Mae said.

"It got me in the —"

"I can see where it got you," Mae said, opening the first aid kit. "Don't poke at it."

"I was in the middle of something important."

"You were in wet grass next to the wood pile in snake season," Mae said. "After I mentioned copperheads twice."

"I was having a revelation."

"You were having it in the wrong location." She looked at the bite, made her assessment, stood up, and offered him her hand. "We're going to the hospital. They'll want to look at it. You'll be fine. It's a juvenile by the look of it."

"How do you know it was a juvenile?"

"Because you're still talking," Mae said.

Jeb took her hand and stood up, leaning on her more than he wanted to and less than he needed to, which was his general approach to accepting help. They crossed the yard together toward the car.

"You're not surprised," Jeb said.

"I'm a little surprised," Mae said. "The specific location is new."

"I was going to tell you that I think I might be cosmically significant and then I got bitten in the —"

"Jeb."

"Right. Car."

She got him settled in the passenger seat. Went around to the driver's side. Started the car. Pulled out of the driveway.

At the first light she picked up her phone and made a call.

"Hey, this is Mae, yes, I need to push my eleven-fifteen, can we do one o'clock? My husband had a situation with a snake." She listened. "No, he's fine. Copperhead, but a small one." She listened again. "I know, right? He was walking near the wood pile. Mm-hm. Okay, one o'clock is perfect, thank you."

She put the phone down.

"You rescheduled," Jeb said.

"Pushed to one," Mae said. "You'll be discharged well before then."

Jeb looked at his wife. She was watching the road. She had her situation entirely managed.

"Mae," he said.

She glanced at him.

"I love you," he said.

"I know," Mae said. "I love you too. Don't touch the bite."

• • •

The antivenom made Jeb warm. He was in a bed. There were tubes. The fever softened the edges of the room.

Mae was in the chair beside him. She had her coffee, which the nurses had provided without being asked.

"Mae," Jeb said.

"Mm," said Mae.

"I need to tell you something."

"You've been telling me things for forty minutes," Mae said. "You told me about the Monads, POTENTIALITY, and the Gentleman's Agreement. Twice on that last one."

"The second time was an important clarification."

"It was," Mae said, in the tone that meant: it was not.

Jeb looked at the ceiling, which was doing nothing remarkable. He appreciated this about the ceiling.

"The thing I'm trying to say," he said, "is that consciousness isn't produced by the brain. It's more like a receiver. And the receiver is tuned to a particular frequency by the Monad that's running the —"

"Jeb."

"Yeah."

"I know," Mae said.

He looked at her. She was looking back at him with the warm eyes and the dubious smile in their usual simultaneous configuration, but there was something else in it today, something quieter that had been there a long time and did not require this conversation to be there.

"You know," he said.

"A stone," Mae said, "chucked into a pond makes waves."

She reached over and squeezed his hand. Once, firm. The squeeze of a woman who has said the thing and means it and does not need to elaborate.

Jeb was quiet.

The antivenom hummed in his blood. The ceiling remained unremarkable. From somewhere down the hall, the sounds of a hospital being a hospital: a cart, a door, a PA system with something to say that didn't concern them.

"That's it," Jeb said. "That's exactly it."

"I know," Mae said.

"You've always known."

"I've always known," Mae agreed. She stood up, smoothing her jacket with the brisk efficiency of a woman who has completed one task and is orienting toward the next. "You're going to sleep now. The nurse said the fever'll break by dinner. Kev's coming at eleven."

"Where are you going?"

"The waiting room," Mae said. "Donahue's on at nine. I haven't caught it in three weeks."

"You're going to watch Donahue."

"I've been trying to catch this episode since Tuesday," Mae said, picking up her coffee. "They've got a whole panel about women who marry men who don't listen, which I find extremely relevant to my life."

"I listen," Jeb said.

"You listen eventually," Mae said. "After you've finished explaining." She patted his hand. "Sleep. Don't pull at the tubes."

She walked out.

The door swung shut behind her.

Jeb lay in the warm blur of the antivenom and thought about a stone thrown into a pond. The rings moving outward from the point of impact, each one carrying the shape of the original disturbance, growing wider and quieter as they went.

He thought: she's known this her whole life.

He thought: she didn't need a single chapter of any book I've ever written.

He thought: the stone doesn't know it makes waves either. It just gets chucked.

He thought: I should write that down.

He didn't write it down. His notebook was in his jacket and his jacket was on the chair and the chair was further away than his current relationship with vertical motion could reasonably support. He made a mental note. He had learned, over the years, that mental notes made in a mild fever had about a forty percent survival rate.

He closed his eyes.

He slept.

• • •

In the waiting room, Mae found a chair with a good angle on the television. Donahue was just starting. She settled in with her coffee.

She watched Phil work the audience. He was good at it. He actually listened to people.

The panel today was indeed about women who married men who don't listen. Mae found herself nodding at intervals. Not bitterly.

Jeb listened, eventually. That part was true. And when he finally got there, really got there, he heard things that most people missed entirely. The man contained multitudes. He also did not finish his leftovers.

The food preservation sealer came to mind again.

She had been looking at one online for two months. Vacuum seals everything: meats, cheeses, cut vegetables, the leftover portions of whatever Jeb ate two-thirds of and declared himself full. The waste was genuinely troubling. She ran a tight kitchen. She had been raised to run a tight kitchen. She was not at war with Jeb about it, she was never at war with Jeb about anything, it wasn't that kind of marriage, but the FoodSaver had begun to feel less like a want and more like a need.

She made a note in her phone: FoodSaver. Check if the model with the roll cutter is on sale anywhere.

Donahue was getting into it now. A woman in the third row had something to say that clearly Phil had not anticipated and was trying to receive with grace.

She finished her coffee.

She thought: Jeb is fine.

She thought: the fever will break by dinner, and she would bring him something from the cafeteria that he would eat most of and leave some of, and she would think about the FoodSaver, and they would go home, and the yard would still be the yard and the porch would still be the porch and the fence would still have the gap in it where the light came through in the mornings.

She thought: a stone chucked into a pond makes waves.

She thought this briefly, then she let it go and watched the rest of Donahue.

It was a good episode.

Chapter Thirty: Kev and the Pasta

The admissions nurse had called her Mrs. Cunningham, which had taken Mae a quarter-second longer than it should have to answer to, long enough for the nurse to glance up from her screen with the polite uncertainty of someone wondering if they'd gotten the name wrong.

"Yes," Mae said. "Sorry. I usually go by Mae."

"Of course," said the nurse.

Mae filled out the forms. She was good at forms.

She handed the clipboard back and went to find coffee.

• • •

Kev arrived at eleven, later than he'd said and earlier than Jeb had expected. Mae had her own opinion about which.

She had met Kev three times before today. He was the kind of person you felt you'd met more than you had. Old past what his years explained.

He came through the lobby carrying a paper bag with the Sav-A-Lot logo on it.

Mae was standing by the coffee machine.

"Mae," he said.

"Kev," she said. "He's in 214. They're watching him for a couple hours but he's fine."

"I know he's fine," Kev said. "How are you?"

"I have a one o'clock hair appointment," Mae said, "which I am keeping, because Jeb is fine and I have been rescheduling this appointment for two weeks."

Kev smiled. It was a small smile and it had considerable depth behind it. "Good," he said.

"Room 214," Mae said. "Don't let him get too wound up. He'll want to talk about the HyperRen thing."

Kev's eyebrows moved slightly. "He told you."

"He was going to tell me right before the snake intervened." She picked up her coffee. "I already knew anyway."

"Did you."

"He's been Jeb for as long as I've known him," Mae said. "Whatever a HyperRen is, it sounds about right." She picked up her coffee. "I'll be back at two. Make sure he eats the lunch."

"I will," Kev said.

Mae collected her purse and her keys and walked out through the lobby. The automatic doors opened for her. The day outside was bright.

Kev watched her go.

He thought: that woman is not confused about a single thing.

He thought: Jeb has no idea how lucky he is.

He corrected himself: Jeb knows exactly how lucky he is. That's half of what makes him a HyperRen.

He picked up his Sav-A-Lot bag and went to find room 214.

• • •

The room was institutional beige. Outside the window, a parking lot. In the corner sat a chair the color of a committee's decision. Jeb was sitting up in the bed with his leg elevated.

"Snake," Kev said, sitting down.

"In the —"

"Mae told me."

Kev settled into the chair. He set the paper bag between his feet. "You figured something out. Before the snake."

"I think I'm a HyperRen."

Kev nodded. Not the nod of new information. The nod of information confirmed.

"You already knew," Jeb said.

"I suspected," Kev said. "You can't confirm it for someone else. They have to get there. Also I wasn't certain. It's not a thing with a bright line." He looked at Jeb. "How does it feel?"

Jeb thought about this seriously.

"Like I found a pocket I didn't know I had," he said. "And there was a map in it. That I apparently put there."

"That's about right."

"And then a snake bit me in the —"

"Yes."

"Is that meaningful? Cosmically?"

Kev considered this. "The snake was doing its snake business," he said. "You were in its coordinates. The meaning is: stay out of wet grass near wood piles in snake season." A pause. "Although."

"Although?"

"The timing does have a quality." Kev permitted himself the small smile. "You were not going to get too large for your yard. Something was going to make sure of that. Might as well be a snake."

"Aplomb," Jeb said. "Even the snake is Aplomb."

"Everything is Aplomb," Kev said. "Or can be. The snake brings you back to the specific. You are not a cosmic entity having a revelation. You are a man in wet grass who needs a hospital. Both are true. You hold both. That's the whole thing."

• • •

"What do I do with it?" Jeb asked. "Knowing what I am."

"What you've been doing," Kev said.

"That's it? That's the wisdom?"

"That's the wisdom," Kev said. "Write the books. Say it almost seems to be. Sit on the porch with Mae and watch the light do things in the yard. Let the raccoon be a raccoon." He leaned forward, elbows on his knees. "The moment you start being a HyperRen instead of Jeb, you stop being either one. The whole reason the large things can hear you is that you're genuinely here. In this. In the hospital room with the bad chair and the parking lot window and the leg that a snake had opinions about."

Jeb was quiet.

"Mae scheduled her hair appointment," he said.

"While you were being admitted."

"I know."

"That's a woman who knows what's real and what's not urgent," Kev said. "She didn't need to sit here and hold your hand. She knew you were fine, and that you'd be better with a couple hours to think without her watching. And she'd been putting off that appointment." He sat back. "She's further along than either of us, honestly."

"Don't tell her that," Jeb said.

"She knows," Kev said.

Jeb looked out the window. A man in the parking lot was having a complicated interaction with a parking meter, which appeared to be winning. The sky above the parking lot was doing nothing remarkable and everything correctly.

"The void has no satisfied customers," Jeb said.

"No," Kev agreed.

"And here always works out."

"Here always works out. Eventually. After an unreasonable amount of time and at least one avoidable mistake."

"I feel like the snake was my avoidable mistake."

"The snake was your avoidable mistake," Kev confirmed, with great warmth.

• • •

Kev stood up. He retrieved the Sav-A-Lot bag from between his feet.

"What's in the bag?" Jeb asked.

"Pasta," Kev said. "The Sav-A-Lot on Millbrook has twenty-five percent off all dried pasta. Ends today at six."

"You came to the hospital and then you're going to the Sav-A-Lot."

"I came to the hospital first," Kev said. "The pasta sale has been running all week. I had time. You were the time-sensitive item."

"I'm touched," Jeb said. "Genuinely."

"You should be," Kev said. "I could have gone to the pasta first. The twenty-five percent was not going to wait for you to get bitten by a snake." He picked up his coat. "Mae's bringing lunch at two. Eat all of it. She'll ask the nurse if you didn't."

"She will absolutely ask the nurse."

"Also." Kev paused at the door. He had the look he got when he was about to say something he'd been sitting on. "Jeb."

"Yeah."

"My mama named me Kev," he said. "But my name is also Ren."

The room was quiet.

"Yeah," Jeb said. "I figured."

Kev smiled. The full one, the one that didn't come out often. "Write the books," he said. "Say it almost seems to be. Watch the yard. Let Mae keep being Mae."

He raised his hand in a small gesture. Then he shuffled out through the door.

The door closed.

Jeb lay back.

Outside, a regular Tuesday was happening in a regular parking lot. The man with the parking meter had apparently reached a settlement, and the sky and the light were what they were.

Jeb reached for the notebook Mae had hung on the chair back before she left.

He opened it.

He wrote: *it almost seems to be.*

He looked at it.

He added: *and that's exactly right.*

He closed the notebook.

He waited for Mae.

At one o'clock she would be getting her hair done, which mattered. At two o'clock she would walk back through the hospital door with lunch and a new haircut and the dubious smile and the warm eyes, and he would love her the way he had always loved her.

He thought: this is it.

He thought: this is all of it.

He thought: the raccoon already knows this.

He thought: so, apparently, does Mae.

★ *The Porch: The Lawn Can Wait*

The lawn needed mowing.

Mae was aware of this. She was sitting on the porch with her second cup of coffee, and the lawn was right there in front of her.

Jeb had left two hours ago with his good jacket on and that particular expression he got when he was trying not to look like he thought something significant was happening. He'd kissed her on the top of the head and said he'd be back by three, which she would believe when she saw it. Big Bert's Bible and Book Emporium ran on its own sense of time. So did Jeb, especially when people started asking him questions, which they would, and he would answer them, at length.

She did not mind this about him; she had decided not to, approximately thirty-two years ago, having learned early on that the thing you accept becomes a door and the thing you resist becomes a wall.

The lawn would get mowed.

At some point before it became a philosophical statement.

A mockingbird landed on the fence post, ran through four other birds' best material, seemed satisfied, and left. Mae watched the space where it had been for a moment.

Jeb would come home and find her here and say something about the lawn, by way of acknowledgment, because he was not actually evasive about the lawn, just chronically optimistic about when he would get to it. She would tell him she wasn't worried about the lawn. He would look at her slightly sideways. She would mean it. He would make dinner, probably.

This was a life.

Mae held her cup with both hands and felt the warmth of it through her palms and looked at the yard: the long grass, the gap in the fence where the light came through at this angle and went golden on the far edge of the lawn, the place near the old oak where the ground stayed damp even in August, the corner where the raccoon had been living last spring and then wasn't anymore, which had mildly concerned her until she found the evidence of a family in progress behind the shed.

Everything was, on the whole, alright.

She had not always known this. There had been years when alright had felt like a consolation prize. But somewhere along the way she had stopped requiring the yard to be different than it was. The grass would grow and the light would come through the gap and the coffee would go cold.

She let it go cold.

A car went by on the street. Someone's radio, briefly. The mockingbird came back, did one new thing, left again for good.

The unmowed lawn breathed in and out in the small wind.

It occurred to her, not for the first time, that most of the wisdom she had accumulated in her life had arrived looking exactly like this: sitting on a porch on an ordinary Tuesday while her husband was at a book signing he would describe for three days. Not thunder. Just a Tuesday that turned out to have something in it.

She thought about the afternoon in October. The three of them at the gate. Ren taking a sandwich and looking at it, Archimedes asking for a third with proper manners, Junior holding the coffee cup. Jeb still thought it was a particularly vivid dream. Mae knew it was lunch.

She thought about Jeb, specifically about his face this morning when he'd put on the good jacket. The particular brightness. The slight additional height he carried when he thought he might, today, be talking about something that mattered to someone who hadn't heard it before.

He had earned that brightness.

She was proud of him quietly. He knew, and that was enough.

The coffee was cold. That was fine.

Mae looked at the gap in the fence where the light was already shifting, the gold going softer.

She thought: *well.*

Just that. The whole thought, complete.

Well.

She would stay here a little longer.

The lawn could wait.

Chapter Thirty-One: The Big Pow Wow Barbecue

It started as a ping.

This ping came from the side. From someone standing at the fence line with a plate of something.

Junior felt it.

He had been sitting with the thing he'd learned at the beach, not thinking about it, but holding it the way Ren held the tear: present without gripping. The beach had given him a willingness to be where he was without needing to be somewhere else.

The ping arrived at the edge of this willingness and sat there.

It had a quality Junior recognized and could not place. Warm, specific, slightly carbonated.

• • •

There were four of them.

He could feel them before he could see them. They were standing at his barrier comfortably, without agenda, with food.

The barrier between Junior and everything else had been, for most of his existence, a wall. Thick, defensive, the architecture of a being who had been burned by other Monads, burned by the Movies, burned by the void. It had softened at the beach. It was no longer a wall. More of a membrane.

The light was right.

Junior looked through the membrane and saw a picnic table.

• • •

It was a picnic table. Wooden, slightly weathered. The kind with the attached benches that require a specific maneuver to get your legs under.

There was a checkered cloth on it, red and white.

There were corn and ribs, potato salad of a quality that suggested someone had opinions about potato salad and had acted on them, and sweet tea in a pitcher beaded with condensation.

Mae had done the potato salad. Junior knew this without being told.

Kev was at the grill. Of course Kev was at the grill. He had the tongs.

Jeb was already sitting at the table with a Diet Fresca, comfortable, with the ease of a man who was not going to help with the grill because helping with the grill was Kev's job.

Ren was setting out plates. Each plate placed with quiet deliberateness.

Junior looked at them through the membrane. They looked back.

"Well," Mae said, in the direction of the membrane. "Are you coming or not? The corn's getting cold."

• • •

Junior went through.

Not with the force of a Monad breaching a barrier. He went through the way one steps off a porch into a yard: one step, ordinary, the membrane parting around him.

The warmth hit him immediately, the warmth of an afternoon, of corn and ribs and potato salad and four people who were glad to see him.

He sat at the table. The bench-maneuver was, as predicted, slightly undignified. Nobody commented. Jeb handed him a Fresca.

"You look better," Kev said, from the grill, without looking up from the ribs.

"I feel better," Junior said.

• • •

Then they reached across and got Archimedes.

It was Ren who did it. Ren had been the one who was always carrying and never carried. He reached through whatever distance Archimedes was on the other side of and brought him over.

Archimedes arrived ruffled, the dignity of an owl who has just been transported without prior consultation.

He looked at the table, the corn, the four beings around it, each one radiating the specific quality of accumulated depth wearing comfortable clothes.

"Quite right," Archimedes said.

Mae put a plate in front of him.

• • •

They ate, talked, and laughed. Kev told a story about the first time he'd tried to cook in a body and had burned water, which Mae said was not physically possible, which Kev said was exactly the point, which Jeb said he could confirm having witnessed it across at least two cycles, which Ren said he believed completely because he had once burned rice so badly that the pot had to be buried in the yard, which Archimedes said was nothing compared to what Junior had done to an entire galaxy the first time he'd sneezed.

Then Kev put down the tongs.

"So," he said.

The table went quiet.

"We're a family now," Kev said. "All of us. That's what this is."

He looked at Junior and Archimedes. "You two have the raw power. The cosmic scale. The ability to generate worlds, to move fields, to do things that none of us in our particular forms could do in a thousand lifetimes."

"And we," Mae said, with the calm of a woman who has been waiting for this part of the conversation and is pleased to have arrived at it, "have more horse sense than both of you put together."

Nobody argued. Junior, specifically, did not argue. He had spent an eternity learning things the hard way, and one of the things he had learned the hardest was that Mae was right about this. His agreement was not required.

"The power without the sense makes a mess," Jeb said. "We've all seen the mess. We've been the mess. The sense without the power is beautiful but small. What we have, together, around this table, right now, that's neither."

Ren was quiet for a moment. Then: "I spent a long time being small and beautiful," he said. "It was enough. But enough and everything are not the same thing. And I think

—" he looked at Junior, "I think we might be ready for everything."

Archimedes ruffled his feathers. "I have been ready for everything," he said, "since considerably before any of you noticed."

Mae handed him another piece of corn. "We know, dear," she said.

• • •

What happened next was not a decision. Six beings who belonged together arrived at the same table at the same time with the same willingness.

Junior and Archimedes, between them, had the generative power of two Monads who had been through enough to know what power was actually for. Kev and Jeb and Mae and Ren, between them, had the accumulated horse sense of hundreds of particular lives lived all the way through, with all the mornings and the grief and the cold coffee and the warm specific human weight of it.

Together, around that table, with the remains of the barbecue and the condensation on the sweet tea and the checkered cloth, they did something new.

They made a world.

Not by the vast imposing itself on the particular. By collaboration. The power serving the sense, the sense shaping the power. They made a place where the windows let the outside in.

The world they made was not perfect. It had conflict and loss and the specific friction of a shared reality where nobody gets exactly what they want, along with weather and bureaucracy and property disputes and catering situations that Darlene would have opinions about.

But it was better.

Kinder, gentler. The windows were bigger. The light came through differently. The people in it would still struggle and still learn. But the ground beneath them would be steadier.

The 2080 timeline.

Ren would come forward, with a different name, in a new century. He would build a company and argue about windows. Some part of him would remember, in his hands, that buildings had to let the world in.

They would live in it together. All of them. Not remembering exactly, because the Movie requires not remembering exactly. But close. Closer than any of them had ever been.

• • •

The barbecue was over. The corn was finished. The sweet tea was warm and the Fresca was flat and both were exactly sufficient.

Mae stood up from the table. She looked at the six of them.

"Same time next cycle?" she said.

Kev smiled. Jeb raised his Fresca. Ren nodded. Junior, for the first time in his existence, felt something he could only describe as: at home while still being somewhere.

Archimedes looked at the table, at the remains, at the checked cloth, at the six of them together.

"Splendid," he said.

The membrane closed gently behind them as they went, each one, toward their place in the new world. A screen door. The kind that lets the air in.

Epilogue: 2080

Ren Corp, São Paulo North Campus, Thursday Afternoon

The sky over the north campus was a saturated blue, the result of atmospheric adjustments the international accord had been implementing since 2061. By any meteorological measure, it was a beautiful afternoon.

Ren Corp occupied twelve buildings on the north campus, of which Building Seven was the oldest and the most beloved, having been constructed in 2041 when Renson himself had still been alive to argue with the architects about the windows. He had wanted more of them. The building had more windows than buildings of its generation typically had. On afternoons like this one, the interior filled with São Paulo light. The plants along the corridor walls had responded to this light by becoming, over the decades, considerably more enthusiastic than plants in office buildings generally were.

The party was in the Building Seven atrium. Renson had built it: a central gathering space large enough for the whole campus but warm enough for two people. The atrium had high ceilings and a glass roof and the São Paulo light coming through it at four in the afternoon made everything in it briefly gold.

Archie's send-off had started at three.

It was now four-fifteen, and nobody had left.

• • •

The hologram occupied a space near the far window, where the afternoon light came in at the best angle and where, in 2041, Renson had put a chair that was still there, occupied now by no one in particular, just a chair doing its job of being somewhere to sit if you needed to.

Archie stood, or what passed for standing in the holographic sense, near the window, holding what appeared to be a cup of tea. It was not real. The cup was not real. The holding was real.

He flickered slightly when the facilities director walked through him on the way to the catering table. 'Quite all right,' he said, without looking up from the tea. The facilities director said 'sorry, Archie' and kept walking.

Archie was old. He had been at Ren Corp since the beginning, not as an employee exactly, since the employment categories available in 2041 had not been adequate to describe what Archie was, and had been, for thirty-nine years, what the company called its Senior Continuity Advisor.

'Yes,' he had said, when Ada called to tell him. 'Shall I make tea?'

He was looking around the atrium.

• • •

Kevin was telling the story about the raccoon.

He was always telling the story about the raccoon, in one form or another. The specifics changed depending on the audience and the occasion and how many glasses of the sparkling thing he'd had, but the essential shape was consistent: enormous being, garbage can, proof in the garbage, the raccoon's complete editorial indifference to the proof. He had been telling this story for as long as anyone at Ren Corp could remember, which was as long as Ren Corp had existed, and the story had acquired, over time, the quality that the best stories acquire: it was true every time you heard it, and it was slightly truer than the last time. Sometimes, in the telling, he would pause at a point that didn't seem to require a pause, and his eyes would go briefly to a distance that was not in the room, and anyone watching closely would have said he was remembering something that sixty-one years did not fully account for. Then the pause would end and the story would continue and the moment would pass, but it would leave behind a warmth in the room that had nothing to do with the São Paulo afternoon.

He was currently telling it to a small group near the catering table. They were laughing in the right places. He was performing with the specific relish of a man who loves a story that has earned its laughs, leaning forward, hands moving, the particular animation of someone who is not describing an event so much as inhabiting it again. He had gray in his hair and lines around his eyes that deepened when he laughed and he laughed often. He was sixty-one years old and had the quality of someone who had been, over the course of his sixty-one years, increasingly willing to be exactly where he was.

He was Ren Corp's Chief Narrative Officer, which was a title he had invented himself and which Renson had approved without asking what it meant, on the grounds that Kevin doing something was generally reason enough for it to be done. What it meant was: he told the story. The company's story, the founders' story, the story of what Ren Corp was for and why it mattered and what Renson had understood that most people hadn't. He was very good at this, and had been, in one form or another, for longer than his sixty-one years fully accounted for, in ways he had never tried to explain and didn't intend to.

• • •

Jeb was by the window.

He was always by the window, or the door, or the edge of whatever space he was in. He gave the room his full attention without asking the room to return it.

He was watching Archie.

He had been watching Archie across years, returning each time and finding something he hadn't seen before. There were moments, brief, unreliable, gone before he could hold them, when watching Archie felt like recognizing a companion from somewhere he had no word for. A table, corn, the specific quality of a checked cloth in afternoon light. He did not mention these moments to anyone, including Mae.

He was Ren Corp's Chief Design Officer. He designed the spaces: the buildings, the campuses, the interior configurations that made the company feel, to everyone who spent time in it, like a place that had been thought about. Jeb was constitutionally opposed to spaces that prioritized being looked at over being inhabited. He designed in the inhabitable sense.

He had been responsible for the windows in Building Seven. He and Renson had agreed about the windows.

He watched Archie accept a glass of something from a passing colleague and do the thing Archie always did with offered things: look at it with genuine consideration, as though the glass itself were interesting, before drinking it. Jeb had been watching Archie do this for twenty years and had never gotten tired of it.

'You're going to miss him,' said a voice beside him.

Mae had extricated herself from Darlene and found the window.

'He's not dying,' Jeb said.

'No,' Mae said. 'Just going somewhere new.'

Jeb looked at the room. At Archie with his holographic tea. At Kevin reaching the punchline of the raccoon story, which Jeb had heard more times than he could count and still found himself leaning slightly toward. At Darlene redistributing catering items with the authority of someone who considers the current arrangement suboptimal and has decided to address this.

"He's always been somewhere else," Jeb said. "Partly." He paused. "Do you ever get the feeling that we've all been somewhere else? Together? Not here. Before here."

Mae looked at him. She had the expression she got when Jeb said something she had been thinking and hadn't said.

"Yes," she said. The same way she'd said it thirty years ago on a different porch, to a different version of the same question.

Mae considered this. 'Is that why you all work the way you do? That thing the company has. I've tried to explain it to people and I can't quite—'

'The windows,' Jeb said.

'Sorry?'

'Renson wanted more windows. Everyone thought it was an aesthetic preference. It wasn't.' He paused. 'He wanted more ways for the outside to come in. He said a building that forgot it was surrounded by a world was a building that was going to start thinking it was the world.' He turned from the window. 'We build the way we build because the world is bigger than the building.'

Mae was quiet for a moment. Then: 'Renson sounds like he was interesting.'

'He was the best of us,' Jeb said simply. 'He just happened to also be the founder.'

• • •

There was a man near the service corridor entrance, large, jacket sized along generous lines, explaining something to a facilities technician about thresholds, with a carburetor in his jacket pocket.

The biplane appeared at four twenty-seven.

It came in low across the glass roof of the atrium. It made a slow, unhurried pass.

Ada saw it. She tilted her head slightly and watched it cross the glass ceiling.

Kevin saw it. He paused mid-raccoon-story and watched the biplane cross the glass.

Archie saw it. He watched it from inside his holographic form.

Darlene saw it. "Huh," she said, to no one in particular, and continued redistributing the dessert situation.

The large man did not see it. He was facing the facilities technician, who had taken out a small notebook. He produced the carburetor from his jacket, set it on a side table to make a point, picked it back up, shook the technician's hand, and moved toward the service corridor.

The atrium returned to being the atrium.

The glass roof caught the last of the biplane's shadow and let it go.

• • •

The speeches happened at four-thirty, when the light through the glass roof had reached its best angle and the atrium had filled to its quiet capacity. Ada spoke, and Kevin after; both were short and kind, and Archie listened.

Jeb did not give a speech. He had prepared something and had decided, standing at the window twenty minutes before the speeches started, that what he had prepared was good but not right. Instead, when Ada looked at him and raised her eyebrows, he simply raised his glass. Archie raised his holographic glass in return. The room understood.

Then Archie spoke.

• • •

'I am going to the South campus,' he said. 'I am going because the South campus does not yet exist as a place, and I have some experience with helping things become places. I have learned, over time, that this requires one thing above all others: someone who is willing to be there. Not to manage it from a distance or model it in advance and implement the model. To be there, in the particular, in the specific morning with the specific light, and to let the place tell you what it needs.'

He looked at the room. All of them, in the gold afternoon light.

'You have been,' he said, 'an extraordinary thing to have been part of.'

He raised the holographic cup.

'Splendid,' he said. He meant it.

• • •

The party continued past its official end. The agenda was finished. People were glad to be in the same room.

Darlene had reorganized the dessert situation to her satisfaction. She was now in a conversation with Ada about

Ada's upcoming visit to Bahia, which Darlene had opinions about, specifically regarding a restaurant near the old market. Ada was writing down the name.

Kevin had found Archie near the window. Their conversation was years old. Nothing needed establishing anymore. Kevin was leaning against the wall. Archie was standing, the hologram's version of standing.

'You could stay,' Kevin said.

'I could,' Archie agreed.

'But.'

'There's a campus that doesn't know what it is yet.' He looked out the window. The sky was going from the saturated blue toward the first colors of evening, which in São Paulo were extravagant by any standard: the atmospheric adjustments had done something to sunsets that the scientists described in technical terms and everyone else described by standing outside and watching. 'I remember what it's like not to know what you are. I have some patience for that condition. More than most.'

'You were good at it,' Kevin said. 'Not knowing.'

'I was catastrophically bad at it,' Archie said pleasantly. 'I was simply persistent.' He turned the holographic cup in his hands. 'That turns out to be sufficient, in the end. You don't have to be good at the unknowing. You only have to stay in it long enough.'

Kevin was quiet for a moment. Outside, the trees were doing something with the evening light.

"He would have liked this," Kevin said. Not specifying. He didn't need to. Then, quieter: "Archie. Do you ever feel like we've done this before? Not this party. This —" he gestured at the space between them, at the quality of the evening.

Archie turned the holographic cup in his hands. "Frequently," he said. "I have attributed it to good design."

Kevin laughed.

Archie looked at the room. At Jeb by the window, watching the evening arrive. At Darlene transferring the entire dessert arrangement to what she had determined was a more logical configuration. At Ada laughing at something the facilities director had said. At the gold light on the walls of the room that Renson had built with more windows than rooms usually had.

'He did like it,' Archie said. 'He built it.'

• • •

Jeb found the raccoon at five-forty.

It was in the catering area, behind the table with the desserts that Darlene had reorganized, medium-sized and entirely self-possessed, conducting a quality assessment of what the rearrangement had left accessible: a small plate of artisanal cheese puffs.

Nobody knew how it had gotten in. The campus had environmental integration protocols that were specifically designed to manage the boundary between the building interiors and the campus grounds, which were themselves a managed habitat with a documented population of urban wildlife that the facilities team tracked and, within reason, coexisted with. The protocols were good. They were not, apparently, infallible.

The raccoon looked at Jeb.

Jeb looked at the raccoon.

The raccoon completed its assessment of the cheese puffs, reached a conclusion, and took one. It ate.

Jeb did not call facilities. He stood and watched, and felt the specific warmth of recognizing a thing he had always known, arriving again in new form. For a moment, the atrium was not an atrium. It was an afternoon. There was a table with six of them around it. Someone had made potato salad. Then the moment passed, and the raccoon took another cheese puff, and the atrium was ordinary again. The warmth stayed.

The raccoon finished the cheese puff. It shook once. It looked at the room, taking inventory. The gold light on the walls. The people in the good conversation. Darlene redistributing the desserts. Archie near the window. Kevin laughing. Ada watching her company.

Then the raccoon turned and moved back toward wherever it had come from.

The atrium continued being the atrium.

The coffee, on the side table near the window where someone had left it an hour ago, had gone cold.

This was fine.

• • •

At six-fifteen, when the sky over the north campus had gone from saturated blue through the São Paulo sunset and arrived at the deep that comes after, Jeb and Kevin found themselves standing on the building's exterior terrace with the remains of their drinks.

The campus grounds were settling into themselves, the lights coming on in the other buildings. Somewhere in the managed habitat beyond the fence, something moved along the perimeter.

'He'll be fine,' Kevin said. About Archie, about the South campus, about the configuration of things moving into new configurations.

'He'll be better than fine,' Jeb said.

Kevin looked at the campus, at the lights in the buildings, at the sky, which was still doing something worth watching, and at the movement along the perimeter that was almost certainly what it appeared to be.

'You know what I keep thinking about?' he said.

Jeb waited.

'That the coffee is cold.' He looked at his glass. 'We have a device. In the break room. The one Darlene sourced. It keeps things at exactly the right temperature for hours. Nobody uses it.'

Jeb was quiet for a moment. The campus settled around them. The sky continued.

'Nobody uses it,' he agreed.

They stood with this together. The silence between them was an old one.

The evening was warm. The light at the edge of the campus was doing something interesting near the fence. Neither of them mentioned this.

The raccoon was working the perimeter. It reached the corner of the fence, paused, conducted its assessment. Found the situation: acceptable.

Moved on.

Before You Go

You made it to the porch. That means something.

If this book gave you anything worth keeping, a scene that stuck, a moment of recognition, a sentence that arrived when you needed it, I'd be grateful if you'd leave a few honest words on Amazon. Independent authors don't have publishers pushing doors open for them. A review from a real reader is how we find each other.

Search for Kevin Cann where you got this book.

About the Author

Kevin Cann is a philosopher, writer, and former nuclear engineer. He is the creator of Platonic Surrealism, a philosophical and metaphysical framework. He co-wrote Chapter 3 of How to Think Impossibly with Dr. Jeffrey Kripal, with whom he has also co-taught at the Esalen Institute. He lives in California.

• • •

For the complete and current list of books by this author, search for Kevin Cann where you got this book, or visit platonicsurrealism.com

For free stories, essays, and whatever arrived since this book went to print, join the author at platonicsurrealism.substack.com

www.ingramcontent.com/pod-product-compliance
Lightning Source LLC
LaVergne TN
LVHW091114080826
845145LV00008B/1918

* 9 7 8 1 9 7 1 8 5 3 0 6 2 *